PRESTER JOHN

PRESTER JOHN

AFRICA'S LOST KING

RICHARD DENHAM

A catalogue record for this book is available from the British Library.

ISBN 978-1-913762-10-0

Copyright © 2020 Richard Denham.

This edition published in 2020 by BLKDOG Publishing.

www.blkdogpublishing.com

EST. 2019

BLKDOG

To my son Tristan.

To my friend Carol who has put up with me and my riddles
all these years.

To all those who have taught me, supported me and
inspired me, thank you.

Se wo were fi na wosankofa a yenkyi.

INTRODUCTION

He sits on his jewelled throne on the Horn of Africa in the maps of the sixteenth century. He can see his whole empire reflected in a mirror outside his palace. He carries three crosses into battle and each cross is guarded by one hundred thousand men. He was with St Thomas in the third century when he set up a Christian church in India. He came like a thunderbolt out of the far East eight centuries later, to rescue the crusaders clinging on to Jerusalem. And he was still there when Portuguese explorers went looking for him in the fifteenth century.

He went by different names. The priest who was also a king was Ong Khan; he was Genghis Khan; he was Lebna Dengel. Above all, he was a Christian king who ruled a vast empire full of magical wonders: men with faces in their chests; men with huge, backward-facing feet; rivers and seas made of sand. His lands lay next to the earthly Paradise which had once been the Garden of Eden. He wrote letters to popes and princes. He promised salvation and hope to generations.

But it was noticeable that as men looked outward, exploring more of the natural world; as science replaced superstition and the age of miracles faded, Prester John was always elsewhere. He was beyond the Mountains of the Moon, at the edge of the earth, near the mouth of Hell.

Was he real? Did he ever exist? This book will take you on a journey of a lifetime, to worlds that might have been, but never were. It will take you, if you are brave enough, into the world of Prester John.

CHAPTER ONE: AN

AFRICAN ROMANCE

FOR BOYS

1910 was one of those golden years before the Great War, when the British Empire still covered vast areas of the world, atlases and globes were covered in British red and Edward VII was the King-Emperor over an unchanging and unchangeable world that was basking in peace and prosperity.

That was certainly how the British aristocracy and the well-to-do saw things. Allowing for a different view of the world map, so did their opposite numbers in the other great powers. France was a proud Republic, still basking in the memories of 'La Gloire' under the first Napoleon. Germany was a new nation, flexing its military and industrial muscles in every sphere of progress and activity. Austria-Hungary was a vast Hapsburg empire, as it had been for centuries, its capital of Vienna the loveliest in Europe, perhaps the world. Russia was the biggest empire of all, thousands of miles of All the Russias, presided over by the Romanovs, who had ruled for three hundred years. Ottoman Turkey dominated the Balkans, linking south-eastern Europe with the mysteries of the fabulous East. The United States was the new kid on the block, as the Americans themselves said, a little brash perhaps, short on history and culture, but a vibrant, cosmopolitan society, hard-working and ambitious. It all looked rather lovely.

Actually, it was not. In reality, it was, as the playwright Alan Bennet said in *Forty Years On* (1968), 'wars and rumours of wars, just like any other time'. If we take the lid off any of the countries and empires listed above, we see worrying signs of concern. Signs that 1910 was a year of flux, of uncertainty, of apprehension. In America, Bert Williams became the first black entertainer to be given equal billing with whites on Broadway in the Ziegfeld Follies, but that was an anomaly and in stark contrast to the continued existence of the white supremacist Ku Klux Klan that encouraged membership of the 'good ol' boys' whose grandfathers had lost the Civil War. The Immigration Amendment Act of 1910 added paupers and the sick to those not welcome on Ellis Island; the 'huddled masses' were being weeded out.

And the Bible belt was widening and tightening. Horrified by the laxity of Hollywood and the 'filth' being pedalled in jerky black and white film reels at cinematographs all over the country, the Christian Endeavor Society of Missouri launched a crusade to ban movies that showed unmarried couples kissing. Many were horrified too, at the tango craze that hit the States that year. When Jack Johnson, the black heavyweight boxing champion retained his title against Jim Jeffries in Reno, Nevada, rioting broke out and ten people died, with hundreds more injured. Over 32 million Americans still lived on farms in the modern, technology-filled twentieth century. Less than half the population had a high school education; only four per cent graduated from college.

The Ottoman Empire had been called the 'sick man of Europe' since the 1850s. When the ineffectual government, the Porte, did nothing to stop the massacre of Christians in the empire in the 1870s, William Gladstone, leader of the opposition in the British House of Commons, demanded that the Turks be 'kicked out of Europe, bag and baggage'. His nemesis, Benjamin Disraeli, supported the Turks against Russian aggression from the north; but in the Balkans, a mish-mash of ethnic, religious and political dissidents, there were increasingly loud demands for reform and even independence. When European war *did* break out in the summer of 1914, it was on the heels of two years of fighting in the Balkans and the murder of Austrian Archduke Franz Ferdinand at Sarajevo in Bosnia.

Russia was in trouble. Tsar Nicholas II, his wife, four daughters and son, had visited England the previous year, staying with George V, the new king now that Edward 'the peacemaker' was dead. It was the last time they were seen outside Mother Russia. Dissidents had sown discord in this vast, peasant-ridden society that adopted western technology and work patterns too late. In 1905, a 'dress rehearsal' for the revolution of 1917 had led to thousands of deaths. Men, women and children marched to the Tsar's palace at St Petersburg to demand improvements to their poverty-stricken lives. Nicholas was not there and a panicky guard opened fire on them, killing hundreds. Devious Socialists squabbled among themselves, dividing into Bolsheviks (the majority) and Mensheviks (the minority), demanding that councils called soviets be set up to replace the Tsar's hated autocracy and secret police.

Austria-Hungary also suffered from being too large and was riven with ethnic dissidence. The ageing emperor, Franz Josef, continually clashed with the Magyars (Hungarians) in his empire and with the Balkan peoples, as anxious to throw off the Austrian yoke as they were the Turkish. As the prime mover in German affairs, Austria had lost her place in the war with Prussia in the 1860s and would never regain it. Like Russia and the Ottoman Empire, Austria-Hungary was tottering. It was associated with a past that did not understand democracy or nationalism but clung to some vague folk-memory of the Holy Roman Empire, that Napoleon had famously destroyed in 1806 on the grounds that it was not holy, nor Roman, nor truly an empire.

While Austria-Hungary was anxious to hold an old empire together, Germany was anxious to create a new one. The foremost imperial power of 1910 was Britain and Britain became the German target. In terms of industry, and of an arms build-up, it became a race for supremacy. The fact that the rulers of Britain, Germany and Russia were cousins counted for nothing. National pride and ambition overruled family relationships. The German navy, the Kreigsmarine, was determined to build more battleships of the Dreadnought class than the British and they already had the numerical edge in submarines. In terms of geography, the only place on earth still ripe for colonisation was Africa and the scramble for that continent kept the colonial office in Berlin on its toes constantly. Sabre-rattling went hand in hand with this expansionist policy and the Germans were very good at it.

The rise of Germany just across the Rhine certainly rattled France. The countries had fought over Alsace and Lorraine in 1870-1 and French pride was left seriously dented. To illustrate the modernity and technological capability of Germany, the army could transport its troops to the Front via twenty-six railway lines; the French had one! Long before 1910, the search for allies was on and so desperate was France that they threw in their lot with Russia, with which they had no affinity whatsoever and, via the Entente Cordiale of 1904, with Britain, their old enemy of a thousand years. Internally, the country witnessed an attack on the corruption and wealth of the Catholic church and was split down the middle over 'l'affair' involving the framing of a Jewish army officer, Alfred Dreyfus, for spying. It exposed France as a state riddled with anti-Semitism (along, it has to be said, with most other European countries).

Britain on the surface looked far more positive than the other powers. The days of condemnation of the British empire, as a prime example of racist exploitation, lay in the future. The reforming Liberal Party had recently introduced sweeping changes – the creation of Labour Exchanges (the forerunner of Job Centres); additional power to the trades unions; a national insurance scheme to alleviate poverty. It was the start of the welfare state which marked Britain as the most forward-looking and caring of the European powers – and streets ahead of the Americans who some would argue remain, to this day, uninterested in equality.

But under the surface, there were rumblings. The international socialist movement of Communism found a welcome reception among the working class and riots among coal miners and steelworkers increased, the government having to utilise police and even the army to restore order. It did not pass unnoticed, especially by the police, that a central figure in all this, Vladimir Ilyich Ulyanov, known as Lenin, spent over a year living in London between 1902 and 1903. In 'John Bull's other island', Ireland, the move for independence increased in violence. The cultural Irish Republican Brotherhood, committed to a resurrection of all things Gaelic, became the Irish Republican Army, with a far more political – and eventually murderous – agenda. With a more peaceful approach, Mohandas Karamchand Gandhi had formed his Indian Home Rule movement, determined to bring about the end of the Raj and take back the jewel in the crown.

And even when the British establishment appeared in all its certainty, we now know how flaky it was. On 23 November 1910, a mousy little American, Hawley Harvey Crippen, was hanged at Pentonville for the murder of his wife, Cora, who trod the music hall boards as Belle Elmore. The case was a sensation, if only because it was the first time that the new technology of radio had caught a killer. Crippen fled to Canada aboard the SS *Montrose*, with his lover and secretary, Ethel le Neve, posing as his son. He had left the remains of Mrs Crippen under the floor of their cellar at 63, Hilldrop Crescent. Inspector Walter Dew of Scotland Yard responded to the radio communication of a suspicious *Montrose* captain and, taking a faster ship, arrested Crippen on board. The forensic evidence against Crippen, as presented by pathologist Dr Bernard Spilsbury, was overwhelming and Crippen hanged (Ethel le Neve being acquitted). In 2002, Spilsbury's notes and slides from the original case were tested by forensic specialist Bernard

Knight. He saw no sign of the famous operation scar by which Spilsbury had identified Mrs Crippen. Neither did the remains in the Hilldrop cellar match any of the 'Elmore' family's DNA. In fact, the buried corpse was that of a man.

In this one small macabre spotlight on an old crime, we have exposed at once the pomposity and brittleness of Britain in 1910. In common with all the other powers in Europe, the country was like a ticking time bomb. And time was running out.

What Britain needed in 1910, as at so many other times in history, was escapism. Enter a minor civil servant called John Buchan and the novel he wrote in this year, *Prester John*.

Buchan was thirty-five at the time. Born in Perth, Scotland, he was the son of a Free Church minister, educated at Hutcheson's Grammar School and Glasgow University before going on to Brasenose College, Oxford, where he won the Newdigate Prize for poetry in 1898. He settled on the law as a career and was called to the Bar in 1901, the year that Queen Victoria died and the country was up to its neck in a war with the Boers in South Africa that was not going well. In the same year, he became private secretary to Lord Milner, the high commissioner for South Africa and spent two years working under him. Milner was a brilliant scholar and diplomat, his most recent appointment as governor of Cape Colony. During the Buchan years, his brief was extended to include the Transvaal and Orange River Colony and he received a viscountcy for his difficult work by 1902.

It was no doubt his time in Africa that inspired Buchan to write *Prester John*, although the novel has little bearing on the fabled immortal emperor who is the hero of *this* book. Back in England, Buchan became a director of the publishing house Nelson's. His first literary work was a collection of essays, *Scholar Gypsies*, while he was still at Oxford. His penchant, however, was for fast-moving action stories, a rather more adult and up-market version of the 'ripping yarns' written for public schoolboys. His best known character, the spy Richard Hannay, was yet to come, *The Thirty-Nine Steps* in 1915, followed by *Greenmantle* in the following year.

Buchan's predecessors in the literary genre were George Henty who died in the year that Buchan joined Alfred Milner's staff and Buchan's own contemporary Henry Rider Haggard. Both men had impossibly pure 'boys' own' heroes, able to sort out rascally natives with their fists, as learned at Eton or Harrow (to which neither of them actually went!), fighting for king and country and saving wilting damsels on the way. Haggard in particular had an appeal because of his African novels. *Cetewayo and his White Neighbours* was a serious factual book about the Zulu king who had destroyed the 24th Foot at Isandlwana in 1879 and was it barely noticed outside Africa. *King Solomon's Mines*, however, was a different proposition. It had a fine, upright chap as its hero, Allan Quartermain, but it also fed into the moody mystery of the Dark Continent, linking it with the ancient world of the Old Testament. It was followed by the equally over-the-top *She* in 1887 and the public loved it.

Prester John was – and is – a gripping read. As testimony to its power, an editor I know remembers as a twelve year old girl reading it sneakily under her desk when she should have been concentrating on her Maths lesson! Buchan would have been delighted. The storyline has little to do with the legendary king who is the focus of this work. As a lowland Scot, John Buchan usually had Scotsmen for heroes; in this case, it is David Crawford who, on the death of his father, goes to work in Blaauwildebeestefontein as a shopkeeper. Here, he meets the dodgy Portuguese trader Henriques and the enigmatic African, Laputa. He picks up rumours of diamond smuggling and, more ominously, a planned uprising by the Bantu tribes, the Zulu and the Swazi, against British rule.

Laputa stirs up unrest and meets his people in caves wearing the ruby-encrusted necklet of the great Prester John himself, which gives authority to his claim to be the leader of his people. Crawford joins forces with Captain Arcoll of the colonial police and ends up being captured by Laputa. The Scot escapes, taking the magic necklace with him and in the denouement, discovers that Laputa has strangled Henriques. He gives chase and Laputa, his rebellion in ruins, commits suicide by throwing himself off a bridge.

Ignoring the complexities of the strained relationships between British colonial rule and the native population, Buchan produces a simplistic thriller which leaves no doubt as to whose side he – and by definition, the reader – should be on. It was literally a black and white world in 1910 and no one seriously questioned that. What Buchan also did, however, was to touch on the mysticism of Africa – ruby necklets, caves, Prester John himself spoke to a world that, for most of Buchan's readers, might have been on the far side of the moon.

Prester John was only the most enigmatic concept to come out of Africa.

CHAPTER TWO: THE

DARK CONTINENT

Today there is nowhere in the world that we do not know about. Some geographical regions are remote and inaccessible, but they have been mapped, explored, photographed and, some would say, well and truly exploited in the name of progress. It was not always like that. When John Buchan wrote *Prester John*, South Africa was only just coming into existence. It had only been fifty years, a single generation, since explorers like Livingstone, Burton, Speke and Baker had risked their lives searching the heart of Africa, travelling beyond the Mountains of the Moon to see what lay beyond.

In the ancient world, North Africa became a Roman province. The most powerful and successful empire in ancient history thrust out from the city of the seven hills in all directions, in search of land, raw materials and power. Long before the European powers scrambled for Africa in the late nineteenth century, Rome held sway from Mauretania in the west (today's Morocco) to Egypt in the east. Between these two provinces were Numidia, Africa Proconsularis and Cyrene, all of them becoming Rome's bread basket. There were few raw materials that the Romans could use, but the plains were fertile where there was no desert and no less than six hundred cities flourished across North Africa in the first century AD. In the centre, today's Libya, stood three great cities whose ruins still stand as a silent testimony to Rome's greatness. Sabratha, Oea and Leptis Magna were huge – the last has the biggest chariot-racing circuit in the world, now at the edge of the sea. The city was the birthplace of the emperor Septimus Severus.

By the time of Nero, in the first century, the philosopher Pliny could claim, without much exaggeration, that six Romans owned all of Africa. Wheat was the major product, as it had been for the Carthaginians before Rome destroyed it in the 120s, before moving south to take the whole of Numidia. When Julius Caesar fought King John of Numidia in 46BC, the area produced 50,000 tons of wheat a year. A century later, the yield was ten times that. Two thirds of Rome's needs were met by this, the rest coming from Europe. So vital was wheat from North Africa that the Romans banned the growing of anything else. There were to be no vines or olive groves, especially as this would impact on Italy's own output of these commodities. A century later, this too had changed, the area by Trajan's time (early second century AD) producing grapes and olives. We know from an inscription in Tunisia in this period, that tenant farmers had to pay of third of their wheat, a third of their barley, a quarter of their beans, a third of their wine, a third of their oil and a sixth of their honey in taxation. If that seems excessive, they still had plenty left over for themselves and to sell at the market.

And as the empire grew, there was a need for Roman Africa to increase in size too. Tertullian, son of a Carthaginian soldier, wrote in the second century, 'smiling estates have replaced the most famous deserts, cultivated fields have conquered the forests, flocks of sheep have put wild beasts to flight'. But the wild beasts were important. If there were two things the Roman loved, as Juvenal said, it was '*panem et ludi*', bread and circuses. Africa provided both – the lions, wolves, elephants, even giraffes that died in the arena to the delight of the crowd; and the less dramatic, but more vital, food supply.

As elsewhere in the empire, Roman ruins are everywhere. El Djean in Tunisia was once Thysdrius, with the largest amphitheatre on the continent. Dongga had originally been a Carthaginian settlement; it had temples to Jupiter, Juno and Minerva. Constantine's aqueduct still follows the natural contours of the Atlas mountains in Algeria, bringing water to a parched land.

We do not know how far south the Romans penetrated. From Frezzan, the territory changes from rocky waste to the Sahara where nothing grows. Early in the second century, two military expeditions marched through this land, held by tribes dominated by the Garamontes to the territory of the Ethiopians, perhaps as far as Lake Chad. They went in search of slaves, ivory, precious stones, rare timber, ostrich feathers and gold. Already, by the second century, there were rumours of fabulous wealth in Africa, items glimpsed briefly in small quantities in the southern markets. And already, as is the way of the world, such things were *just* out of reach.

To the south of the Roman frontier lay the Sahara, the home of the nomadic Berbers who drifted from oasis to oasis with their flocks of sheep, goats and camels. To the south west was the empire of Ghana, made up of tribes whose cultural and religious centre was Timbuktu. They controlled the western Sudan and the Senegal valley. The combined geographical barriers of the desert and the Atlas mountains probably slowed trade development here, as African climate and geography still hamper progress today. The West African world opened up in the eighth century, by which time Islam had flooded the area with a fanatical devotion to Allah and a thirst for conquest every bit as determined as that of the Romans.

Ghana was actually the name of the empire's warrior king and he may have been a proto-Prester John in his own right. The forests and savannah that he owned produced iron ore, ebony and ivory. It also produced gold that was ferried up the river Niger to Timbuktu, which may explain the origins of the legendary mines of King Solomon. Salt was traded from the flats of Taghaza and Idjul and Mediterranean glass, pottery and oil-lamps made their way downstream to the city of Jenne-Jeno, already one of the largest in Africa by 200AD.

By the eleventh century, the Arab geographer al-Bakri claimed that, at Jenne-Jeno, the king's dogs wore solid gold collars. By the fourteenth century, when tales of Prester John were already linked with Africa, another geographer, Ibn Khaldun, believed that the Ghanaian king owned a lump of solid gold that weighed a ton.

The inhabitants of the forests of Ghana were black Africans formed, by the tenth century, into a confederation of tribes of the Soninke peoples. The Muslim tribes further north were the paler-skinned Berbers, of mixed Negro and Indo-European descent. These were the original people of North Africa and from the first century BC withstood waves of invasion by Romans, Vandals and Byzantine Greeks. Their nomadic lifestyle probably made them largely immune to this colonization, their long, low black tents as common now in the twenty-first century as at any time in the past.

The Berbers were nominally converted to Islam by Abd Allah ibn Yasim who travelled the Sahara in the 1030s. He was not popular, often on the run and ended up setting up a rabat, a religious commune, near the estuary of the Senegal river. They came to be known as the Almoravides, a growing number of religious zealots who invaded already Muslim Spain fifty years later. Ibn Yasim was killed in a raid in 1059 and the northern part of Almoravid territory was controlled by Yusuf ibn Teshufin, a semi-literate, unstable character who drank only milk and ate only barley bread. He smelt and his Arabic was poor but he was a fine general and systematically conquered what is now Morocco throughout the 1070s.

Unlike the earlier Islamic invasion of Spain by Tariq (after whom Gibraltar is named – jebel al Tariq was Tariq's mountain) the Almoravides brought Allah with the sword. Conversion was essential; refusal to comply meant death. In the mantra of Islam – 'There is no god but Allah and Mohammed is his prophet'. Twice in three hundred years,

Africa had come to Europe. The various Islamic dynasties that ruled North Africa had a bloody reputation, but in essence, they were the successors of the Romans. The Almoravides dominated the north-west, modern Morocco with its cities of Fez and Marrakesh. As their rule died in the 1140s, the Almohads took control of central North Africa, today's Tunisia and Libya. Tunis, Tripoli, Algiers and Barca were their principal settlements. In Egypt, always a rather different prospect because of its long, sophisticated cultural history, first the Fatimids, then the Ayyabids and finally the Mamelukes held sway between 909 and 1517.

The problem with trading further south was first the Sahara, the vast desert that stretches from Egypt to Morocco. Stand at the foot of the pyramids in Giza and look westward and you are staring at three and a half million square miles of sand. The Tuaregs who controlled the desert by the Middle Ages were notorious bandits. They attacked camel caravans and left corpses under the merciless sun as a deterrent to others.

By the thirteenth century, the Almohads had travelled up the Nile, establishing trading points far beyond the usual area known to the ancient Egyptians. Later generations of Europeans, mostly British, became obsessed with searching for the source of the Nile, but Medieval man used the river for food and trade, not academic achievement or international glory. To the eastern bank of the river lay Nubia, a Christian kingdom and south of that, along the horn of Africa that provided the Red Sea's coast. From here, traders crossed the continent westwards, across the Sudan, increasing the importance of the tribes here, first Ghana, then Mali. These peoples traded, above all, in gold, the indestructible metal which was *the* hallmark of legendary wealth. In 1324, the Mali king Musa went on a pilgrimage to Mecca, taking so much gold with him that the economy of Cairo collapsed. An atlas produced in Catalan Spain in 1375 shows Musa sitting on his throne with a crown on his head. He holds an orb and sceptre, the symbols of European kingship and of course, they are made of the purest gold.

In the western Sudan, a number of states prospered

because of the gold trade – Takrur on the west coast, Ghana itself between the eighth and ninth centuries. Along what would become, ominously, the Slave Coast by the eighteenth century, Akan, the Yoruba states and Benin dominated, while further north, Mossi, Oyo, Nupe and the Hausa states watched each other warily, their frontiers fluid, their history only partially recorded.

It is a valid criticism of Europe, western Europe in particular, that it has been for centuries totally self-absorbed. Areas outside it are suitable for trade, or conquest, but little else; the United States has inherited this legacy and for all its cosmopolitan make-up, is the biggest culprit of insularity today. While Europe was considered in the fourteenth century, the 'hurling time' because of internecine warfare between factious nobles under weak kings and while it was decimated by the outbreak of bubonic plague, the Black Death, black Africa came into its own in a pinnacle of success it has never reached since. The Kanim dynasty, east of Lake Chad, ruled the region for six centuries, unlike the English Tudors, for example, who only lasted just over one.

Mausa Musa – another living example of Prester John – and Sonni Ali were famous throughout Islam and Christendom for their wealth, power and achievement. Timbuktu and Jenne were formidable cities, with stone buildings and walls, universities that attracted Islamic scholars and poets. They used a mixture of diplomacy and military force, exactly like the kings of Europe. They had sophisticated bureaucracies that enforced their laws and taxed their people.

But these African kingdoms, largely but not exclusively Muslim, had no urge to extend beyond the coasts of their continent. Africa was too big and too diffuse, region by region, to form a coherent whole. We have seen that by 1910, the big European empires were in serious danger of breaking up to the forces of nationalism and democracy. The rule of thumb was, the larger the empire, the more likely it is to fragment. So it was never possible to create a single state called Africa; even a relatively small area like the Hausa states in the western Sudan never united into a single entity. That weakness, the tribal culture so deeply embedded in the African mindset, was one that could be exploited by a European state that was already united, one that looked outward in the age of exploration which began in the fifteenth century; Portugal.

Medieval scholarship, taught at its zenith in universities from Oxford to Kiev, knew that the world was flat. In an image repopularized by the late author Terry Pratchett, the disc that was the world was carried upside down by four vast elephants that in turn stood on the back of a turtle, paddling its way through the universe. Above it shone the radiance of Heaven and at night, God's light twinkled through the holes in the firmament which we call stars. Magical fiction like this is the stuff of Prester John, but by the middle of the fifteenth century, there were men who began to doubt it. What if the world was not flat, but round? If that were the case, it would be possible to travel west to arrive in the east and vice versa. No one knew how long this would take or what lay, for example, beyond Ireland, despite the fact that the Vikings had undertaken this hazardous journey at least five hundred years earlier. Man's memory is short and, as we shall see in the case of Prester John, legend, hearsay and just plain old nonsense tend to get in the way of truth. We still, after all the counter-evidence of the last half a millennium, have a Flat Earth Society!

And by the middle of the fifteenth century, there was a pressing need to find a new way to the east. In 1453, the Ottoman Sultan Mehmet II became 'the conqueror'. His armies had battered the last stronghold of Byzantine Christendom, the walled city of Constantinople, for months and he at last walked into the great church of Hagia Sofia, threw dust over his head, knelt and gave thanks to Allah for his victory. The monks cowering in the walls' recesses were dragged out and butchered. Hagia Sofia became a mosque (today, it is a museum) and the fall of Constantinople hit Christian Europe like a tidal wave. Worse was to follow. The Ottoman Turks spread ever further north west, coming to within a day's ride of Vienna by 1683. They did not, unlike Mehmet's first conquest seven centuries earlier, insist on conversion to Islam, but they did raid the trade caravans that brought precious spices from the east to the European markets; and the race was on. There had to be another way to reach India and the Spice Islands; European economies relied on it. While Cristoforo Colon (Columbus), Amerigo Vespucci and Giovanni Caboto (John Cabot) sailed west to impossible New World adventures, the Portuguese sailed south out of the Tagus, hugging the west African coast until they could find the continent's southern tip and reached the Indian Ocean.

On the way, the Portuguese could not resist bartering with the locals, about a dozen ships a year from 1480, putting in at the fortress of Elmina. They bought cloth and hardware and received gold from the interior and slaves in return. Today, slavery is regarded by many as the worst evil in history. In fact, it had been the way of everyday life in all the civilizations of the ancient world, from Sumer to Rome. Under the emperors in the second and third centuries, there were four times as many slaves in the city of Rome as free men. The same was true of the African states. *All* of them employed slaves. Men, women and children were taken as prisoners after raids into enemy territory and used as labourers in appalling conditions. We have only to look at inter-tribal warfare in the emergent African states at the end of the twentieth century to see the mindset behind those outrages. There is no doubt that the Portuguese and Arabs and later the British, French, Germans, Dutch and Americans, exploited the situation for their own ends but they did not instigate the system and in several cases brought benefits to the area which African tribes did not.

We must be careful not to cherry-pick our collective history. While there is no doubt the transportation of millions of Africans to the Americas via the Atlantic slave trade was abhorrent, it was by no means unique.

It is a strange phenomenon of our modern world that the Arab slave trade, which devasted Africa, has largely been forgotten. The Africans suffered four centuries of the Atlantic slave trade when tribesmen were sold to Arab traders and then on to British, French and Dutch slave owners in America. In the Americas male slaves were valuable for their physical strength, whereas females had an equal value as breeding stock for subsequent generations.

As the Muslims conquered swathes of Africa, the old gods were replaced with Allah. Islamic law forbade taking a Muslim as a slave; this was not always honoured, but this ironically led to a massive importation of slaves from outside the Muslim world. As more and more African lands fell to Islam, this meant they had to spread their net further south.

We should also be aware that before the arrival of Europeans, slavery was endemic among the native populations. Perhaps what is different is that the Muslims castrated their male black slaves and did not allow them to breed. This had the effect of essentially removing the traces of their crimes because there can be no family stories in the sense of Alex Haley, several years ago, being able to trace his ancestry.

The first of the Portuguese explorers was Bartolomeo Diaz De Novaes, who set sail with two ships in 1487 and rounded Africa's southern tip which he called the Cape of Storms. Beyond that and the Great Fish River lay miles of open sea, the Indian Ocean. Vasco da Gama was next. Ten years after Diaz he commanded the four ship expedition of King Emmanuel I and landed at a point on Africa's east coast on Christmas Day 1497. He called it Natal. From there, he hugged the coast as far north as Malindi, from where he could just make out India's west coast, Malabar. Although da Gama was blameless for later European exploitation in Africa, in 1502 he returned to Calicut on the Malabar coast, sacked the town and moved inland as far as Cochin, going home laden with stolen booty. He was created Admiral of India and became its first viceroy in 1524.

In keeping with the European exploratory mindset, this first wave of discoveries, coupled with the opening up of the West Indies and the Americas, was jealously guarded by Portugal and Spain. By the mid-sixteenth century, the Angolan area around Luanda on the west coast and a long strip from south of Sofala on the east coast as far north as the horn of Africa, was in Portuguese hands. Mozambique, established in 1507, was the most important strategic stronghold. They used the gold of the Zambesi basin to pay for the spices from Goa which were distributed around Europe from Lisbon. Portuguese monopoly of the spice trade was never established and smugglers continued to exploit the wide-open spaces of the Indian Ocean. Nevertheless, for a century after 1500 the Portuguese were largely unchallenged.

Although the Indies were the ultimate target of the Portuguese, the whole of Africa's west coast was explored and mapped by various explorers in the late fifteenth century. The area just south-east of the Canary Islands to Sierra Leone effectively became Portuguese trading territory between 1434 and 1460, largely under the organizational talents of Henry the Navigator. Not an intrepid sailor himself, Henry lent gravitas to exploration because he was the son of King Joäo I and had an extraordinary ability to appoint men who could get things done. The coastal strip from Sierra Leone to Cape St Catherine was the province of Piero de Corvilha in the late 1480s.

In this period, Sunni Ali became king of the Songhay people who lived along the river Niger with their capital, Gao, many miles inland. Ali's large empire was usurped after his death by Askia the Great; it was now that Timbuktu and Jenne became centres of Muslim culture. South of the Niger, the Portuguese traded with the Hausa city states and the Dyola who dominated the Mali and Songhay tribes. By 1500, Benin and Oyo emerged as the leading producers of African art, the famous Benin bronzes and terracottas.

The peoples inland from the coast were experiencing a cultural and economic break-out in the early sixteenth century. What was essentially an agricultural community based on cattle was fast appropriating iron and copper. From 1484 when the Portuguese anchored in the mouth of the river Congo, they found the powerful and cultured kingdom of Luba and Lunda, Bantu-speaking peoples who themselves had links to the heart of Africa, unknown to any white man.

While Diego Cao plotted a further stretch of coast from Cape St Catherine to Cape cross by 1485, Fernao Gomes was busy sailing back from Calicut and Goa on the Malabar coast of India. Not only did he chart the route which later became the shorter, overland way to India under the British Raj, crossing the Mediterranean and the desert from Port Said to sail down the Red Sea, he also put in at Sofala, on the African east coast opposite Madagascar and established the most southerly of the Portuguese trading posts there. It was here that the Europeans met the most impressive of all the African kingdoms, that of the Mwenemutapa people around the river Zambezi. The colossal settlement there had been destroyed several times, by war and fire, but from the fourteenth century a huge stone palace of the king had been built. Its walls were thirty feet high, higher than in most European cities at the time and the fortifications enclosed a temple to rival the Acropolis in Athens. The Zimbabweans (as they are today) traded as far away as China.

One of the many tragedies of Africa is that European involvement brought its own pettiness and rivalries. Islam had already established itself all over the north of the continent as far south as the southern Sudan; and Islam, in its first manifestation at least, had been an alien faith from Arabia forced on the African locals, who had their own gods and culture long before Islam arrived. Christianity was another external force, centred on the Copts of Egypt, the country of Nubia and, some said, the kingdom of Prester John. National rivalries kicked in later. While Spain and Portugal tolerated each other by virtue of having colonial interests in different parts of the world, the Dutch, the British, the French and the Germans all squabbled with each other over who controlled Africa.

What we have in the exploration and development of the dark continent is a thin strip confined to the coast. Not until the Nile was finally traced to its source in the 1870s; not until South Africa was parcelled up between the British and the Dutch; not until France and Germany elbowed each other to grab little bits of territory – German East Africa,

Richard Denham

French Congo and so on; can we say that Africa was fully explored and then, perhaps, only partially understood. In the centre was the heart of Africa, not coloured foreign in Victorian atlases, a heart that had beaten for centuries but without a sound because of a total lack of written culture.

Although it is disputed today, central Africa was, for over 100 years, assumed to be the birthplace of man, where hominids, as opposed to apes, made their first appearance. It is ironic that this area, largely south of the Equator, was also steeped in mystery and in many ways, has remained tied to nature in the way that all primitive peoples once were. Technology barely touched it.

We know from geology and archaeology that south of the Sahara, long before the arrival of the white man, tribes were hunter-gatherers who only slowly embraced an agricultural way of life based on wheat and barley. The idea probably came from Asia across the narrows of the Red Sea and cultivation radiated outwards from the fertile plain of the Nile basin. From here westward, a broad band of savannah and grass Steppelands extended to the west coast. The southern Sahara, in what is now the Sudan, was once far more temperate – harpoons made of bone have been found here, implying a fish economy based on rivers or swamp. The Sahara's desiccation began in the third millennium BC, pushing its inhabitants east to the Nile or south into the centre. About 4000BC we find remains of settlements that ate millet and sorghum. Yams were common in west Africa, where tropical forests, thick and impenetrable, made the creation of fields almost impossible. It may be that by 500BC, wandering tribesmen had moved down the Rift Valley from Ethiopia into what is now Kenya and Tanzania.

By the fourth century AD, we have clear evidence of tribal warfare, not unlike that in Europe. While waves of Vandals, Goths and Huns were swarming over the collapsing Roman empire, the Kushite state south of Egypt was overthrown by Axim, a rival peoples in northern Ethiopia. Axim had a maritime trade in ivory by this time and the Axim fleet dominated the Red Sea, until it, in turn, was overwhelmed by Islam in the seventh century.

Iron came to central Africa via the Nile to Merre, probably by 500BC and from the north-west empire based on Carthage. Soon after this, black farmers established themselves in the Congo basin. They were the Bantu and became the dominant peoples of Africa rather as the Celts were in Europe. Much of the research that has gone into early and Medieval Africa is based on linguistics because of the lack of written record. It is less than satisfactory and in the gaping holes left in our knowledge, legends like that of Prester John can take hold and grow.

In terms of cattle-raising, archaeological discoveries of animal bones enable us to plot the development of organized farming over millennia. It spread further south as the geology and climate of the regions changed and the Sahara and Kalahari deserts became a reality. By 1500BC, cattle were being farmed as far south as the Equator, but they were unknown in the far southern region of the Drakensberg Mountains until 1000, shortly before the crusading era in Europe and the Middle East and about the time that Viking exploration began in the New World.

Sketchy as our knowledge of the heart of Africa is, Europeans in the past knew nothing of it. In 27BC, the squint-eyed geographer Strabo arrived in Alexandria, Egypt, on the staff of the Roman governor, Gaius Gallus. Rome had recently destroyed the empire of Cleopatra, last of Egypt's pharaohs and her lover, Marcus Antonius (Shakespeare's Mark Antony) and the Romans were keen to cash in on Egypt's wealth. To call Strabo a geographer is being more than kind. Faculties of this sort did not exist in the schools, even of the scholarly Greeks and when Strabo wrote about the Nile, it was a mixture of uninformed observation and tittle-tattle picked up from Roman, Alexandrian and Egyptian sources.

He was told, as he sailed in his galley upriver, that the Nile itself was sacred – the multitude of shrines on both banks was testimony to that. The Egyptians were a simple, inbred, superstitious people where incest was the norm. Men urinated sitting down; women did it standing up. At Arsinoe, Strabo visited Crocodilopolis, a shrine that worshipped the sacred reptile. The animal was called

Petesuchos and ate meat and drank wine given to it by visitors. It wore gold 'earrings' and bracelets on its forefeet.

Many miles away from Crocodilopolis was Praenoste, a town near Rome. In a mosaic in a sanctuary there is an imaginary depiction of the Nile. 'Imaginary' is not the right word; it is a realistic attempt to incorporate all the tall stories of the river and its people. The banks crawl with lions, giant centipedes, camels and animals which have no name. Towers and temples stand mid-river where in reality there was nothing but water and the occasional sand-bar. On the banks, there was an almost complete reversal of the Roman norms of behaviour. Men stayed at home three thousand years before the concept of 'paternity leave' and 'house husband'; it was the women who bartered in the market-places. The looms operated in reverse to Roman and Greek frames. Men carried heavy loads on their heads; women on their shoulders. Men did not support their aged parents, their sisters and wives did. Men had two sets of clothes; women only one. Women carried their babies for fewer weeks than their European counterparts; twins and triplets were more common than singeletons. Pigeons laid twelve eggs rather than the customary two. Most goats gave birth to five kids. In the mudlands of the Nile lived creatures that were half mice, half sand.

Fast forward nineteen centuries. In 1881, the explorer, writer − and, some said, sex maniac − Richard Burton, wrote, 'Madness comes from Africa'. He was one of an extraordinary group of Englishmen who risked their lives in the 1860s and '70s to chart the interior of the dark continent and in particular, to find the source of the Nile. Strabo's Romans got nowhere near it and it is testimony to the wildness and hostility of Africa's climate and geography that it took Burton and co. all those centuries to travel further. Twenty years earlier, another explorer, Samuel Baker, wrote to his sister, 'My magnetic needle directs me to Central Africa'.

Unimpressed by legends of Prester John or King Solomon's Mines somewhere near the Mountains of the Moon, hard-bitten men like Baker nevertheless suffered from 'Nile fever', a contagion found among many members of the Royal Geographical Society at the time. With his wife Florence (whom he had bought in an eastern European slave market!) Baker set off from Cairo in April 1861. An inveterate hunter (his favourite gun, 'Baby', has survived), Baker shot and ate crocodile and hippopotamus. The natives ate the animals' lungs, liver and kidneys raw. Naked little boys swarmed all over his boat, begging for alms for Allah. The temperature was 110°F. The Nile 'was as thick as pea soup and not only undrinkable but unmashable'.

The Greek philosopher Herodotus, the 'father of history', had described the source of the Nile, as he believed accurately, in the third century BC – 'The springs of the Nile flow between the two mountains, Croplii and Moplii and the springs are bottomless; half the water flows to Egypt and the north; the other towards Ethiopia and the south.' The Bakers were trying to prove Herodotus right or wrong and to get there they had to hack their way, using swords and axes, through the Sudd, river reeds taller than a man. Their steam-boat engines packed up and they had to hire black labour to drag the vessel with men up to their waists in water.

Recurring malaria and severe sunstroke, which almost killed Florence, were the least of the Bakers' worries, but they found the Lake of Dead Locusts, from which the great river flowed and Baker knelt at the water's edge and thanked God.

What Baker had done, along with Burton, John Speke, David Livingstone and a handful of others was to further the cause of geography and science and to provide proof. What they also did, unwittingly, was to destroy the magic and the mystery of the dark continent. There were no King Solomon's Mines. Egyptian women did not urinate standing up. Sand-mice did not exist. The Mountains of the Moon were here, on earth; opinion is still divided as to their exact location, with some saying Mount Kilimanjaro is the real location, others the Mount Abuna Yosef area in the Amhara Region of Ethiopia.

And was there ever, could there once have been, the kingdom of Prester John?

Richard Denham

CHAPTER THREE: THE

LION OF JUDAH

F ive years after Samuel Baker set off with 'Flossie' in search of the source of the White and Blue Nile, John Camden Hotten wrote a book called *Abyssinia or the Land of Prester John*. After all the stories of the man in the Middle Ages, the consensus of opinion was that it lay in north-east Africa with Kenya to the south, the Sudan to the north-west and the Red Sea to the east. To the south east lay Somaliland, occupied by the British who were keen to secure their strategic coaling station at Aden across the Gulf as part of their world-wide naval supremacy. In the years ahead, Italy, a new nation in 1861, embarked on an imperial adventure in Somaliland as part of the scramble for Africa.

The country was mountainous, especially to the north, with sudden ravines, some 4,000 feet in depth. The rivers, including the Abbai or Blue Nile, were only navigable by small, native craft. They were particularly prone to flooding in the rainy season (June-October) and became virtually dry at other times. Irrigation was therefore difficult and agriculture rather hit and miss.

Abyssinia was always cosmopolitan, the core

Abyssinian tribes living in the centre north of the modern capital Addis Ababa. Their language was Semitic, but subdivided into dialects so different they were almost separate tongues. In the Gojjani region, to the south-west of Lake Tsana, the language spoken was Hamitic. There were small groups of Bantu in the south and a sizeable, though alienated, population of Jews known as Falasha, as well as Arabs and Indians who operated as merchants along the Red Sea coast.

The political structure of the country was complicated, as was the area's religion, but almost before anyone in Western Europe was aware, Britain went to war with Abyssinia.

The king of Abyssinia, a latter-day Prester John perhaps, was Tewodros II, known to the British press as 'Mad King Theodore'. As historian Ian Knight says in *Go To Your God Like A Soldier*, 'The British had a habit of crediting their opponents with mental instability, presumably because of the presumed insanity of challenging the Empire in the first place.' There can be no doubt, however, that Tewodros was highly irrational, almost bipolar in the context of policy, especially concerning foreigners. In that sense, he was merely the first in a long list of African dictators, right up to Idi Amin in the twentieth century and Robert Mugabe in our time.

The French consul at Gondar in 1864 was Guillaume le Jean, who knew Tewodros as well as any European. The king was 49 at the time, of average height with quick, darting eyes that missed nothing. He invariably wore a military cassock, trousers and a girdle and carried a British-made sword. On the march, which he often was against interlopers or rebels in his own kingdom, he carried a soldier's plain black shield. Trotting on foot beside his horse was a page who carried the full-dress version, of blue-velvet with Napoleonic fleur de lys. His official correspondence with the British government was stamped with a royal coat of arms, a lion counter-passant (lying down and looking over its shoulder) and the words *Moa ambasa zaoemoeagada Juda* (the lion of the Race of Judah has triumphed).

Tewodros claimed to represent the Coptic Christians in Abyssinia, determined, in the flowery language of le Jean to 'destroy Islamism and raise the Cross above the Crescent'. Any wavering from the peculiarly Abyssinian concept of Christianity was met with imprisonment and death. In January 1861, in putting down a rebellion by Negousié, a local chief, Tewodros promised sanctuary to all those who deserted the rebel. Hundreds did. Tewodros cut off their hands and let them die of thirst. He told his clergy, the powerful churchmen who were the only literate group in the country, that 'I have made an agreement with God. He has promised not to come down upon the earth to smite me and I, on my part, have promised not to ascend to heaven to molest him there'. No wonder the British press called him mad, although the few more 'snowflake' souls of the time might have discovered that, in the twelfth century, Henry II of England made similar threats against Heaven. All that did was not to defend Tewodros and belittle the English heritage, but to convince the newspaper-reading public that the king was barbarously Medieval at best.

To be fair to Tewodros, he was trying to modernize Abyssinia and invited British, French and German envoys to help him from his sumptuous court at Magdala. When little actual help was forthcoming, Tewodros threw his toys out and threw a number of missionaries into gaol. Britain demanded their release, which the king ignored. The late 1860s was arguably the start of 'gunboat diplomacy', although technically the phrase 'imperialism' was not coined by the British government until 1874. An army was raised, largely in India with troops geographically nearest to the country and used to extremes of climate, under the command of General Robert Napier.

The Abyssinian campaign was a brilliant success for the British. Thirty years later, the poet Hilaire Belloc wrote of colonial wars like Abyssinia –

> 'Whatever happens, we have got
> The Maxim gun, and they have not.'

The rapid-firing weapon was not invented until 1883, but

British firepower in the form of Lee-Enfield rifles and the discipline behind them far outstripped Tewodros' Medieval army in 1868. In the major clash of arms outside Magdala, the Abyssinians' assaults were beaten back time and again. An estimated 700 of them were killed, with perhaps 1,200 wounded. By contrast, Napier's men had twenty wounded, two of whom died.

In a typical volte-face, Tewodros released his hostages unharmed but refused to surrender. In the assault the followed, the king blew his brains out with his pistol. There were no reprisals. The British took no advantage of the situation and the army went back to India. Twenty years later, it began all over again, but this time, the Abyssinians' enemy was Italy – and the result was very different!

If we look at the land of Prester John through European eyes in the years before the Abyssinian campaign, we have an assortment of Englishmen, Frenchmen and a smattering of Germans who all tried to make sense of the incomprehensible. According to John Hotten, using the memoirs and journals of a number of explorers, the Abyssinians were a deeply conservative and superstitious people. Iron workers, for example, were believed to be able to turn themselves into hyenas and kill people. Over time, there was official state slaughter of these people, equated loosely with the *loup garou* of France, or the *wehr-wolf* of Germany. Morality differed enormously; highway robbery was a commonplace and usually acceptable. So was rape and adultery. There was no attempt to cope with mental illness, as misunderstood in Abyssinia as it still was in Europe at the time. By European standards, houses were filthy. Gambling was unknown. Change of any kind was abhorrent – which explains the various rebellions against Tewodros' attempts to modernize. The people were litigious, taking cases to tribal courts and they could all argue for Africa! They were generous, however, giving gifts freely, even to strangers. Begging was everywhere.

In keeping with the ancient Jewish tradition, Saturday was as important a day as the Christian sabbath in some areas. The goose was unclean, so was the wild boar

30

and the hare, limiting the range of food available. As in Medieval Europe, Christian saints' days proliferated and during them, no work was done.

In the 1860s, the absolutism of the king was falling apart, especially in the north. Here, small tribes proliferated, the chiefs or Ras vying with each other in a way that characterized feudal Europe six centuries earlier. Ten years before this, the British consul in the area, Walter Plowden, left a detailed account of the country which he forwarded to Lord Granville, the Foreign Secretary. The Andorra region was ruled by Ras Ali; Tigré and Samian by Ras Oobeay and the central area of Shoa by Sahela Selassie. Plowden had been appointed by Lord Palmerston, 'this terrible milord' who liked nothing better than to shout at foreign diplomats in English, although he spoke French, Italian, Spanish and Russian! In November 1849, a treaty 'of friendship and commerce' was drawn up between the British government and Ras Ali. The arrangement lasted until 1854, when Ali was overthrown by a palace coup by Tewodros, who promptly tore up the agreement. In the years that followed, Plowden and an earlier explorer, William Bell, were murdered and Captain Charles Speedy, of the Indian Intelligence Service, vanished completely. Working in the land of Prester John was a risky business.

One of the prisoners held by Tewodros that led to the Abyssinian campaign was the Reverend Henry Stern. He worked for the Society for the Promotion of Christianity amongst the Jews and belonged to that school of muscular missionaries who was convinced, along with nearly all European artists of the nineteenth century, that Christ had fair hair and blue eyes; he would, if he had had the chance, no doubt have attended an English public school! The Falashas were regarded by some – as most Abyssinians were – as the lost tribe of Israel from the days of the diaspora of the Old Testament (native American tribes were categorized similarly). Divorced, by language and geography, from the Semitic heartlands, their grasp of all things Jewish was limited and distorted, as was that of their Christian counterparts. Most of Stern's correspondence was written while he was Tewodros's prisoner, but he still had the *sang froid* to deal with everyday matters of Abyssinian culture, dress and behaviour. He was particularly fascinated by female hairstyles 'where curl papers have not yet been introduced'. Special wooden 'pillows' made of carved wood, accompanied women everywhere and were used, not for comfort, but to keep their braided hairstyles intact. Men were no less vain; the Rastafarian 'dreads' which shifted with the 'triangular trade' in slaves to the West Indies, was born in the mountains of Abyssinia.

We have already heard the words of the French consul at Gondar in connection with Tewodros, but he had a great deal else to say about the king's country in the 1860s. He pulled no punches. The patriarch Salama, head of the Coptic Christian clergy was 'haughty, violent, avaricious and a meddler; he spends his time between usury, intrigue and commerce'. He told his confessor (who seemed to be unaware of the sanctity of the institution, in that he told somebody else) that he had nine mistresses, two of whom were nuns! Again, we may be struck by the parallels with Medieval Europe. The description of Salama would fit hundreds of Catholic bishops and above, including the popes, between the tenth and sixteenth centuries. Only a middle class Victorian Frenchman could be horrified by it all.

One of the most detailed accounts of the Abyssinians comes from James Augustus St John, who had travelled widely in Egypt and other parts of Africa and wrote his views on the country in the mid-1840s. He had an artist, Achille-Constant-Theodore Emile Prisse d'Avennes, more commonly known as simply Prisse, with him who, in an age before reliable photography, made detailed sketches of the terrain and the people they met. With more than a nod to prurience, St John described the nobility of the slave girls, who were always sold first in the markets and commanded the highest prices. When St John asked how much a particular girl cost, he was told he could have her in exchange for the double-barrelled shotgun he carried. To paraphrase Rudyard Kipling years later, a woman was only a woman – the shotgun might save St John's life!

To be fair to St John, his motive was to set slaves free

(both Livingstone and Baker in the years ahead did the same thing) but he bit off more than he could chew when he tried to buy a beautiful Galla girl from the south. She carried an ornate dagger which she continually played with and had not been bought for three months, perhaps because traders knew a psychopath when they knew one! St John was fascinated by girls up to fourteen – who wore nothing but a short apron decorated with shells. These were personal ornaments of which they were very proud and refused to be parted from them, not for modesty, but because of the sentimental value of the apron, given to them by their mothers. He was fascinated, too, by the tininess of Abyssinian girls, their hands in particular, and pontificated on the shape of their breasts. This sort of comment was on the very edge of acceptability to the Victorians, most of whom regarded explorers as lecherous goats after the proverbial one thing. When Richard Burton became the first Englishman to translate the Kama Sutra, England was outraged; the man was clearly a beast!

Mansfield Parkyns was another example. Dismissed by the Royal Geographical Society as a mere 'nimrod' (hunter), he spent three years in Abyssinia in the 1840s. Landing, as most explorers did, at Massowah on the Red Sea coast, he hired native bearers and moved inland. The country took its toll of Europeans, if only because of the extremes of temperatures, the raging floods and burning deserts. For three years, however, Parkyns did not even wear a hat!

One of the most bizarre customs of the Abyssinians which had been discussed – and disbelieved by most – by earlier travellers was the eating of *brundo*, steaks from a living cow. Rather than kill the animal and butcher it for meat, various tribes, especially the Gallas, immobilised the cow and sliced off portions from the hindquarters while it was still standing and cooked the cuts accordingly (or not, as the case may be – raw steaks were also eaten). Parkyn's answer to his readers (the book was published in 1853) who found this custom revolting, was that it was no worse that the European practice of crimping salmon or cooking eels and lobsters alive. He also made parallels with the

European past. Abyssinians cut off hands, feet and tongues for various offences 'but this punishment is a mere shadow of the refinement of savage cruelty practised by our forefathers not many generations ago and sanctioned by the laws of an enlightened and civilized nation'. He points particularly to the hanging, disembowelling and quartering of traitors still being carried out by the Stuarts in the seventeenth century.

A well-known traveller in 1841 was Major W.C. Harris who led a Mission to Sahlé Selassie, the king of Shoa. His colourful account of the country's inhospitability fascinated and shocked his readers. The heat was 'a suffocating Pandemonium, where no zephyr [West Wind] fanned the fevered skin; where the furnace-like vapour exhaled almost shocking respiration, created an indomitable thirst and not the smallest shade or shelter existed'. Twenty years later, Napier's soldiers fought a war there in these conditions and all but two of them lived to tell the tale. Harris was certainly over the top, even by the gushing literary style of the time. The sky became 'the molten vault of heaven'. The sun was 'the implacable orb'. Time 'slowly flaps his leaden wing'. No wonder people read Charles Dickens instead! The queen was impressed, however; Harris dedicated his book to her and he was knighted soon afterwards.

The French and Germans both sent expeditions to Abyssinia in the late 1830s, the most detailed account coming from Theophile Lefevre, which was as concerned with geographical and scientific research as it was with commerce and potential exploitation. This was the decade of Charles Darwin's famous voyage to the Galapagos Islands aboard the *Beagle*, a milestone in world exploration. Lefvre's book cost an astonishing £20 (almost £2,000 today) so it is small wonder that few people became acquainted with the strange land of Prester John. He cited fourteen cities as potential markets for European goods and outlined the import-export position. The Abyssinians exported gold, ivory, coffee, musk, wax, rhinoceros, hippopotamus, antelope and buffalo horns, hides and teeth, as well as ostrich feathers, tortoiseshell, gum, myrrh, senna and pearls. In exchange, they imported cloth, woollens, cotton and silk, glassware, earthenware, tin, mercury, scissors, nails, sugar, tobacco, copper, guns and sword blades. Although France was losing the competition with Britain as the 'workshop of the world' by this time, the level of industrial production was still far ahead of Abyssinia, which explains the interchange above.

Rochet d'Hericourt was there at the same time and left an account of Sahlé Selassie, the Ras of Shoa, one of the lions of Judah whose dignity and mystery was still captivating the world when his descendant Haile Selassie appeared before the League of Nations in the 1930s to complain about Mussolini's outrageous attack on his country. 'Sahlé Selassie was seated on a leathern chair ... his head bare and his hair frizzled into little curls, a small gold cross was suspended from his neck by a blue ribbon ... two massive gold bracelets on his wrists completed his costume.

It is from d'Hericourt that we have what had been commonplace by the 1830s – sniping between rival explorers. Some of this was international – the French claiming that Harris's expedition was useless largely because it *was* English. Earlier – and later – we have rivals of the same nationality bickering; Richard Burton and John Speke ended up not speaking to each other and Speke eventually committed suicide over the brutal rivalry.

The Frenchmen Combes and Tamisier in the 1830s were fascinated by Abyssinian music, so different from their own and they transcribed it. They were the folk tunes of Shoa and Gallas, hummed or played by all and sundry. Their work was slammed by Dr Edward Rüppell, an Austrian surgeon who travelled up the Nile from Cairo in 1834. Unlike them, he was a dedicated scientist and Rüppel could not forgive the fact that the Frenchmen were the first Europeans to visit Shoa and Crojan, for two hundred years – and they had missed opportunities. Rüppel's maps however were excellent and all subsequent explorers and missionaries benefited from them.

As might be expected, the Reverend Samuel Grobat reported things from the point of view of a missionary. He travelled largely in Tigré and Gondar in 1832-3 and listed the Christian sanctuaries he found there (which would be ignored by Tewodros forty years later). He clearly disagreed with Rüppel who told him that all Abyssinians were 'rascals, without truth, gratitude or faith'. Grobat tried hard to trace the origins of the Falashas without much success. Some accounts suggested they had come south with Menilec, the son of Solomon of the Old Testament; others contended they settled in Abyssinia after Vespasian put down the Jewish revolt in 70AD.

Grobat was not impressed by Abyssinian morality. He found the people nomadic by European standards and the practice of polygamy clearly unnerved him. That said, for a churchman he was a man of the world and wrote that 'he saw less indecency in the capital of Abyssinia than in the capitals of England, France and Egypt'. And if the Abyssinians were liars, the Arabs were worse, with no sense of shame. Consul Lejean found Grobat too naïve, however. He believed virtually everything he was told.

There was an appreciable gap, chronologically, in the exploratory record of Abyssinia. Henry Salt visited three times and left details from his final expedition, that of 1809-10. He described the African practice of marriage etiquette, which sounds very like the system that had operated in Europe for centuries. A prospective groom applied to his would-be bride's parents for consent and it was all about the size of her dowry in terms of gold, cattle, muskets or cloth. The girl was rarely consulted. The Christian element in all this, of the newly-weds taking communion together as part of the ceremony, was in decline when Salt was there.

He noticed how mean the locals were in providing water. Milk and bread were no problem however so Salt assumed that this may have had some ancient origin to do with the veneration of the sacred waters of the Nile. Much of Salt's narrative was spent sniping at James Bruce, perhaps because the Scot was the first Briton to spend years in Abyssinia and to record what he saw. 'Mr Bruce's account is a gross exaggeration,' Salt wrote, 'not a particle of truth in his statement', 'as false in his deductions as in his premises' and so on. Bearing in mind that all these men, in terms of sociology and anthropology, were amateurs, the vitriol can only have been personal for reasons now lost.

Salt's first expedition to Abyssinia took place in 1805, the year of Trafalgar when a Napoleonic invasion of Britain still looked imminent. One of his crew on board the *Antelope* was a sailor, Nathan Pierce, who jumped ship and stayed in the region of Tigré for five years rather than face the rope had he returned to Portsmouth. He became indispensable, not only to Salt on his return visit, but to the local ruler, Ras Selassie, to whom he became advisor and military general. Pierce never did go home.

Salt first went to Africa as secretary and draughtsman to Lord Valentina in 1802. He described the sudden flash floods which destroyed such roads as existed in minutes and the protocol involved in meeting the Ras at Abha. All visitors had to strip to the waist to prove they were unarmed and could only speak to the man in a whisper, close to his ear and with a mask over the mouth.

But nobody wrote more clearly than James Bruce, nor did any foreigner endear themselves so much to the Abyssinians. The Reverend Grobat forty years later came across people who still revered Yagoube, the Abyssinian version of James. A *lik* or judge, told him that Bruce 'was a learned man ... he was beloved and respected by all the great people of the country'. Like Samuel Baker years later, Bruce was a bear of a man, at 6ft 4in, with a great sense of humour and an indomitable spirit. It helped, of course, that when he arrived in the country in the 1770s, the Abyssinians had never seen firearms and Bruce bristled with them. It must have been a similar situation to that of the Incas and Aztecs and the Spanish conquistadors of the sixteenth century.

It was Bruce who first recorded the *brundo* practice of eating raw meat from the living cow and he was universally disbelieved at the time. He recorded the high incidence of tape-worm, called Farenteit, the worm of the pharaoh, and added that pharaohs were held to be evil genii who once ruled the country. The food took some getting used to – spices like pepper used with such profusion 'as absolutely to blister a European palate'. Alcohol was considered dangerous, not for Muslim religious reasons, but in terms of health.

Bruce wrote about the common practice of selling relatives, which was still going on in Europe in his time. Thomas Hardy's *The Mayor of Casterbridge* years later is based on this premise – a man who sells his wife and feels guilty about it for the rest of his life. Hardy's readership (in the 1880s) was shocked, but he was describing a routine practice among the Irish and Scots navvies who built Britain's railway network fifty years earlier.

Bruce described a number of towns in Abyssinia, especially Adowa, the capital of Tigré, with its cloth production and its Jewish enclave. Axun was the ancient capital and the ruins still stood in Bruce's day. In one square alone were forty obelisks but they carried no hieroglyphics and were clearly Greek in origin. The language of the court and the upper echelons of society was Amharic, but what books there were, were written in Geez, an altogether older language.

Like all explorers, Bruce was fascinated by the protocols of royalty. The king attended church regularly, on foot and heavily protected by a bodyguard contingent. He kissed the threshold and the columns at the church door and the steps that led to the altar. He did not necessarily attend the actual service, but rode back to his palace on a mule – 'Mr Bruce has sometimes seen great indecencies committed by the said mule in the presence-chamber, upon a Persian carpet'! Every day, the palace was woken up by an official called Serach Massery, who wandered the passageways cracking a loud whip, 'worse', wrote Bruce, 'than twenty French postilions' (France and Britain were at war, on and off, throughout Bruce's life). This was to chase the hyenas away and to wake the king, who tried legal cases before going to breakfast at eight o'clock.

In terms of literacy, Abyssinians did not use paper (even though the Egyptians to the north had invented it!) but wrote on animal skins instead, which Bruce assumed was an ancient Jewish custom, as in the lost tribes of Israel (see later).

What horrified Bruce's readers and made them

doubt his veracity, was his description not just of the cow torture banquet, but the orgy that followed it. 'Love lights all the fires,' he wrote poetically, 'and everything is permitted with absolute freedom.' Everybody was in the same room and sacrifices were made, in true scholarly Classical tradition, to Bacchus and Venus. A couple left their benches and the men sitting next to them held up their robes to make a makeshift screen, behind which the couple got on with it. It is not clear from Bruce's account whether this congress was done for his benefit or not. The couple then returned – 'all this passes without remark or scandal; not a licentious word is uttered, nor the most distant joke upon the transaction.'

What horrified Bruce was the scruffiness of the churches. There were pictures all over the walls, painted on parchment 'in a manner little less slovenly than you see paltry prints in beggarly country ale-houses [at home]'.

As we go further back into the discovery of the land of Prester John, the gaps become greater. Charles Poncet was a French doctor who reached Gondar from Khartoum on the Nile in 1698, seventy years before Bruce got there. He had lived for years in Egypt and was invited by the then king of Abyssinia to visit, whether for medical reasons or trade is uncertain.

Before that, the Spaniard Jerome Lobo encountered all sorts of problems in 1624. Obviously, the rarity of European travellers anywhere in Africa presented problems; by the nineteenth century, such visits were far more commonplace. Lobo witnessed the cattle-eating ritual and found the Galla tribes to the south ferocious and untameable, an animal reference which many Europeans used in connection with Africans. No other witness describes the butchery of local children who were born on plundering raids into enemy tribal territory and this may be an example of hearsay rather than eyewitness testimony; it was only a few years before this that many Christian Europeans believed in the blood-libel that Jews routinely ate Christian babies. The king, on the other hand, was kindness itself and swore on the head of a sheep covered with butter that Lobo would come to no harm.

Richard Denham

The royal capital, at Baylin, was a primitive settlement, consisting of twenty mud huts and six tents. In the palace proper, the king shared his apartment with his horse.

As we move back in time through the seventeenth to the sixteenth centuries, we find a different take by the explorers. They are largely Portuguese and usually churchmen, intent on spreading Christianity to those areas of the dark continent where it did not already exist and to correct it where it did to conform to the rigid precepts of Rome. There is nothing remotely scientific or geographical about those early explorers; the natives were little better than heathen animals and their only salvation was to find the Christian God through muscular missionary work.

The problem with these early accounts is that they were not made public. Even the earliest of them took place years after the invention of the printing press, but the idea of African travel was too alien for the European book-buying market and the writings therefore obscure. One of them was not a Bible-thumping missionary but a sensitive soul happy to work with the Abyssinians in their own culture; he was Pedro Paez, a Jesuit missionary from Olmeda, near Madrid. His is only the second description of the eating of raw flesh at banquets and he said it was consumed between cakes (a sort of sandwich two hundred years before such a thing had been 'invented' in England) that were too big to fit the average mouth. This was the job of the servants, to force feed the guests 'as if they were stuffing a goose for a feast'. Paez could not quite believe that there was no crockery or cutlery and the chairs were just the mud floor.

Francisco Alvares, however, was a friar of the old school, sent by the king of Portugal, Manuel I, in 1520 with the specific purpose to convert the Abyssinians to Catholicism. The Catholic church was under intense fire in this period as a result of the Reformation. Three years earlier, the rebel monk Martin Luther had nailed his ninety-five theses to the door of Wittenberg cathedral complaining about the immorality and dishonesty of the church for which he worked. For well over a century, Europe would be convulsed by the fallout from that and the Catholic church attempted to strengthen its hand by taking its creed to the furthest ends of the earth. Two years before Alvares got to Abyssinia, Hernando Cortez was commissioned by the Spanish governor of Cuba to conquer the Aztecs of Mexico and impose Christianity on them. In the same year as Alvares, Francisco Pizarro conceived the idea to smash the Incas of Peru, although his expedition was not launched until 1526. In the light of these men's exploits, perhaps the Abyssinians got off lightly. Alvares was appalled by the feasting, the wine which 'walked about with great fury' and the uncouth behaviour even of royalty. The king was constantly engaged in warfare with rebellious tribes and his capital was actually one enormous army camp, not unlike that of the Ottoman Turks to the north-east. The king was suspicious of Alvares's mission, which, had he known of Cortez and Pizarro, was perfectly justified.

Twenty years before Pizarro, a soldier-missionary, Father Oveido, wrote to the king of Portugal – 'I earnestly entreat you to despatch 1500 men, with which I undertake to conquer all Abyssinia'. It was, mercifully, never acted upon.

Today, John Camden Hotten's book *Abyssinia – Life in the Land of Prester John* would be taken to task under the Trades Descriptions Act. In its 380 pages, he mentions Prester John once:

> 'To the old classic writers of [Abyssinia] it was the land of monsters and terrors. To the learned of the Middle Ages it was the country of Prester John – a land where the mountains were all of pure gold and the children played at marbles with big diamonds ... Men with long tails, ladies with two heads and scores of other wonders were to be met with here. Even the Portuguese travellers who went there could only describe the country as the most horrible and depraved or the most beautiful and moral, which they had ever visited. It seems that there has always been something in the land which prevented a

truthful estimate being formed of it.'

There was no sign, even by the 1520s, of Prester John.

CHAPTER FOUR: LEBNA

DENGEL

There are one or two late examples of books with Prester John in the title, but most of them were published before 1680 and were often one-off examples. The oldest account that John Hotten could find was a book written by John Potken in Rome in 1513. Written in Latin, there were no copies anywhere in Britain in the 1860s.

To be fair to Father Alvares, he did mention Prester John in the published account of his mission in 1540. In fact, he claims to have worked with him. Although details are sparse, the missionary would have travelled to Abyssinia around the Cape of Good Hope on board a caravel, itself developed from a Portuguese coaster. These high-sided ships had two, sometimes three, masts with square sails and fore and aft canvases. They had to be sturdier than their Medieval counterparts because of the rough seas encountered and the lengths of voyages. There had to be enough room for food, ropes, equipment and above all, fresh water. Whether he took a single ship or several is unknown; Alvares's interest lay in the land he visited, not how he got there.

Naturally, as a priest, he was fascinated by the Abyssinians' liturgy and their religion generally. He knew from legend and perhaps Potken's book that they were already Christians, but he found their particular take on the faith very different from that of Rome. 'They pray or chant very loud,' he wrote, 'without art in singing and they do not recite verses but will sing straight on'. Alvares was used to masses in Latin and church music known as the Gregorian chant, the plainsong of eight modes common to the Catholic church in Europe. As Combes and Tamisier discovered in the 1830s, Abyssinian music was very different.

'Their prayers are psalms,' Alvares wrote, 'and on feast days [of which there were many] besides psalms, they recite prose – according as the feast is, so is the prose. They always stand in church at matins.'

Today in western Europe, we are used to wooden pews in older churches, plastic chairs in newer ones. The Medieval style was to stand for the whole of church services and to pray lying flat on the flagstones of the floor with arms outstretched, in acknowledgement of Christ's crucifixion. We do not know if Alvares visited the church of St George, but it still stands today and, by the standards of Portugal, was very different from anything he would have known. It was carved out of the solid rock in the uplands in a pit twelve metres deep. The entrance was in the form of a sloping passage alongside the pit, the equivalent of a European pathway to the church door between the gravestones. The whole building is in the shape of a cross with a flat roof at ground level and a base that looks as if it could be straight out of the twentieth century Art Deco movement. Ten of these churches were built in the thirteenth century on orders from Lalibela, a particularly devout Christian king who, again, may be the origin of the Prester John legend. Freestanding churches like this are found nowhere else in the world and they were probably built by Egyptian Coptic Christians running south from the spread of Islam in the eighth century.

The lessons in the services that Alvares witnessed were read by priests, 'rather shouted than intoned, in the way that, in representing the passion of our Lord, we speak the words of the Jews'. This was a slight criticism, an example of how the beauty of a European mass had been corrupted. 'Their voices being so harsh,' Alvares went on, 'they say it as quickly as a man's tongue can.' By the early sixteenth century, something of this was happening in Europe too, no doubt in Alvares's own Portugal. Illiteracy was high and congregations merely copied the Latin of their priests as best they could. The term 'hocus pocus' which became associated with witchcraft in the same period comes from the Latin communion Mass – *'hoc est corpus'* (this is the body [of Christ]).

Alvares was disparaging of the marriage system, with which of course, as a Catholic priest, he had only the merest acquaintance by virtue of the ceremonies he performed for a bride and groom. 'When they make these marriages they enter into contracts, as, for instance; if you leave me or I you, whichever causes separation shall pay such and such a penalty. If either of them separate, that one immediately seeks a cause of separation for such and such reasons, so that few incur the penalty and so they separate when they please, both the husbands and the wives.' If all this has a twenty-first century 'pre-nup' flavour about it, it did not sit at all well with a Catholic priest, to whom divorce was anathema. It *did* happen in Europe, but only for very serious liturgical reasons (consanguinity, for example) and often with the intervention of the pope himself. 'If there are any,' Alvares wrote, 'that observe the marriage rule they are the priests who can never separate.' This, of course, was the exact opposite of the European stance, where all priests (and nuns) had to be celibate – an insistence, by the way, often ignored. The other group in Abyssinia who tended to keep their solemn vows were the farmers 'who have an affection for their wives because they help them to bring up their beasts and sons.'

The missionary was not just appalled by the casual nature of marriage, he had comments to make on circumcision too. This was 'done by anybody without ceremony, only they say that so they find it in the books, that God commanded circumcision. And let not the reader of this be amazed – they also circumcise the females as well as the males, which was not in the Old Law.'

The 'Old Law' is likely to mean God's command to Abraham in Genesis 17:10 or Leviticus 12:3. Both these mentions refer to male practices only; *female* circumcision was about something else. Three and a half centuries later, Samuel Baker came across the practice when he was Governor-General of the Upper Nile. Little girls had their vulvas partially sewn up so that their later grooms could be sure of their virginity when they married. Baker put a stop to it, but it remains a practice in various Asian cultures to this day, despite Western libertarian outrage in the press from time to time.

Equally horrifying to Alvares was the baptism ceremony through which Abyssinian children were put. In Europe, a priest would mark a baby's forehead with a cross shape, his finger dipped in holy water. He would place salt in the child's mouth to purify it and frighten away the devil. In some parts of Europe, the entire baby was dipped (briefly) in the water of the font. All this was literally child's play by comparison with Abyssinian practices. 'They take a clove of garlic,' Alvares wrote, 'large and moist and place it on the corner of the eye (or wherever they want to make the mark); with a sharp knife, they cut round the garlic and then with the fingers widen the cut and put upon it a little paste of wax and over [this] another paste of dough and bandage it for one night with a cloth and there remains for ever a mark which appears like a burn, because their colour is dark'.

This was an example of scarification, common to most African peoples and had a magical significance which would probably have been lost on the missionary. Such processes took place to mark milestones in life – birth, puberty, marriage and so on.

There were areas in Abyssinia where strangers like Alvares were not allowed to go. At Amba Geson, the prince's mountain, there was a door at the foot of cliffs that led to the summit. Anyone trying to cross the threshold would have hands and feet cut off and his eyes gouged out.

There was, however, no problem in making contact

with Prester John himself. Whether Alvares believed that the regal-looking emperor he was introduced to was *actually* the man of already-existing legend or merely a descendant is debatable. He was actually Lebna Dengel, the nagusä nägäst, the overlord and emperor of Abyssinia who went by a number of names and titles during his lifetime. He believed himself to be a descendant of Solomon, the wise king of the Old testament from the tenth century BC, whose alliances with Egypt established him as a ruler in north-east Africa and led to the legend of his fabulous mines, buried somewhere in the dark continent.

Solomon's reputation was that of a dark king, a great magician who led armies of demons and in that sense, he was a worthy ancestor of Prester John. The boy who would succeed him was born about 1496 in Debre Dano in the Tigré region, the son of the emperor Na'od and empress Na'od Mogesa. On his father's death, Dengel became emperor as Davit (David) II, crowned on 13 May 1508. Since he was only twelve, a regency was set up under his grandmother, the formidable Eleia, well into her seventies at the time. Boy kings were bad news for any kingdom. Both England and France in this period suffered from the problem. Edward V was twelve when he became king of England in 1483; Charles VIII thirteen in the same year. Edward's reign was ended prematurely when he was murdered (one of the 'princes in the Tower') and Charles's reign was a disaster. In the case of Abyssinia, the early years of the sixteenth century saw increasing pressure from the pushy Ottoman Turks. If the country was to preserve its Christian tradition, Eleia would have to work hard to keep the crown safe for Dengel and she did not hand over power to him until 1516, when he officially came of age.

This was essentially how Alvares got to Abyssinia; he was the spiritual arm of the envoy sent by João III, the Portuguese king, that arrived at Massowah on 9 April 1520 under the command of Rodrigo de Lima. There were no roads as the Portuguese knew them and it took the party six months to find a way across the mountains to reach Dengel's camp. The missionary priest described the young man who was either Prester John or his descendant:

'In age, complexion and stature, he is a young man, not very black [!]. His complexion might be chestnut or bay, not very dark in colour; he is very much a man of breeding, of middling stature. They said that he was twenty three years of age and he looks like that, his face is round, the eyes large, the nose high in the middle and his beard is beginning to grow. In presence and state he fully looks like the great lord he is.'

If the contemporary portrait of Dengel by Cristoforo dell' Altissimo is accurate, the missionary's description does not do him justice. His hair is thick and curled in the Rastafarian style, his lips full (as is his beard) and he wears expensive gold earrings. Above all, he looks intelligent. Alvares's comments on the emperor's complexion is an example of the subconscious racism of the time and of the novelty of meeting Africans; he expected them all to be black in common with the West African slaves already trickling into Europe.

With an eye to the main chance, the Portuguese had already thrown in their lot with Dengel. Forming a rough and ready Christian alliance with the emperor against the Ottomans, the Portuguese fleet attacked Zeila and burned it to the ground. Dengel ambushed and killed the Emir Mahfuz of Ahel in the same operation.

Three years later, as de Lima's expedition arrived, the Ottomans launched a new offensive. Ahmed ibn Ibrhaim al-Ghazi, known as the Imam, inherited his father's sultanate in that year and made Umar Din the sultan of Adal. His objective was nothing less than the destruction of the Abyssinian empire. He crossed the Anash River and reached Fatagar in 1528, looting and burning Badege before Dengel could get there with his army.

The Ottoman tactics had changed since their controlled and organized assault on Constantinople in 1453. Now, it was all about lightning cavalry raids and pillage, which actually did nothing to win hearts and bring about Islamic acceptance. Dengel caught up with the Imam's troops in March 1529 and routed them at Shimbra Kure.

It had looked as though the Muslim threat had disappeared six years before this and when the Portuguese arrived, Dengel was less inclined than his grandmother to deal generously with them. The Europeans stayed in Abyssinia for six years and Alvares had many opportunities to see Dengel in action. As his fame grew, as emperor and general, he came to be known as Waneg Segad, 'to whom the lions bow'. It was probably at his palace at Shoa, on the site of the later capital of Addis Ababa, that Alvares saw the processional umbrella, nine feet high and laden with ritual significance. It was the official cover of the *tabat*, the ark of the covenant.

> 'They brought down from the church four large and very splendid umbrellas ... [The Prester] then ordered that they should plant the umbrellas on the ground in the sun like a tent and tell me that when he travelled and wished to rest, either he or the queen, his wife [name unknown], they set up one of these and rested under their shade, or ate and slept if they so desired ... Those umbrellas were so big around that ten men could very well be under the shade of them, all covered in silk.'

Alvares's use of the term Prester is interesting. The word was a combination of priest and elder, which in many religions means the same thing. It is the origin of the Presbyterian element of the reformed Christian church in Europe, run by elders elected from the community, rather than royally-appointed bishops. The tradition of priest-king was ancient and universal. In western Europe, the king was not only the Lord's anointed, he was placed on the throne by God himself. From 1558, the queen of England was also head of the church, however priests argued over the exact form of words involving the euphemism 'governor'. In ancient Rome, from which most European (and some north African) traditions stemmed, the emperor was also *pontifex maximus*, the high priest. And the process worked both ways; in Alvares's sixteenth century, the pope was not only the spiritual father of all Christians, he was a priestling with his own territory, the Papal States, and an army with which to defend it.

One of most important religious festivals that the Prester oversaw was a mass baptism at Epiphany, on 6 January every year. Vast numbers took part, from the humblest subject up to the emperor himself:

> 'In the tank [some sort of giant font] stood the old priest, the Prester's chaplain, who was with me on Christmas night and he was as naked as when his mother bore him and quite dead with cold, because there was a very sharp frost, standing in the water up to his shoulders or nearly so, for so deep was the tank that those who were to be baptized entered by the steps naked, with their backs to the Prester and when they came out again, they showed him their fronts, the women as well as the men.'

No doubt, the missionary was appalled.

One of the oddities that Alvares found in Abyssinia was an exile, Piero da Corvilha, who had been sent on a trading expedition to the Levant (Middle East) by João II of Portugal in 1487 and had ended up in the country looking for Prester John. Alvares clearly spent his time with da Corvilha, who by this time had a wealthy Abyssinian wife, lands and titles:

> 'When he saw that we were ready to leave, a passionate desire to return to his country came upon him. He went to ask leave of the Prester and we went with him and urged it with great insistence and begged it of him. Yet no order for it was ever given. This Piero da Corvilha is a man of great wit and intelligence and there is no one like him at court. He is who knows all languages that can be spoken, both of Christians, Moors [North Africans], Abyssinians and heathens and who got to know all the things for which he was sent. He gives an account of them as though he had them present before him.

For this reason, he is much liked by the Prester and all his court.'

They never did let him go home.

Lebna Dengel underestimated the tenacity of the Ottoman Turks. Three years after his victory at Shimbra Kure, they were back, bringing firearms to the Horn of Africa for perhaps the first time. Gradually, the emperor was driven back into the mountains, never again able to put an army into the field, but forced to fight piecemeal, with guerrilla raids that never win wars. Churches and monasteries were destroyed and Abyssinians forced into Islamic conversion at sword point. Three of the Prester's sons were killed in this fighting, his bodyguard butchered and his treasury looted.

Asking, as his grandmother had, for Portuguese help, Dengel did not live to see it, dying an outlaw in his own land at the monastery of Debre Dano on 2 September 1540. As the Ethiopian historian Taddesse Tamrat wrote in 1972, 'The Muslim occupation of the Christian highlands … lasted for little more than ten years, between 1531 and 1543. But the amount of destruction brought about in these years can only be estimated in terms of centuries.'

Why did the Prester, to whom the lions bow, not let the Portuguese adventurer de Corvilha, go home? Because he liked and valued him, certainly, but also because de Corvilha would have told all Europe about the Prester and his magical kingdom north of the Mountains of the Moon. Dengel's story is no more remarkable in historical terms, than that of any ambitious king in Africa or Europe at the time. But if Francisco Alvares believed that Dengel was the legendary Prester John, he was mistaken.

In the 1520s, Prester John had yet to be found.

CHAPTER FIVE THE TALL

TALES OF JOHN

MANDEVILLE

E ven his name was a lie. He claimed to be a fearless traveller, Sir John Mandeville, from St Albans in England. In fact, he was probably John de Bourgogne, a clerk who never left France. Even that is disputed by scholars today. He himself says in *The Book of Marvels and Travels*, 'I, John Mandeville, knight, although I'm not worthy, who was born in the town of St Albans, set sail on Michaelmas Day in the year of Our Lord 1332 ...'

There are a number of physical reminders of Mandeville – a fresco in the great abbey church at St Albans, the fact that his book was in the abbey's library in the fifteenth century, a tomb in the abbey before Henry VIII's dissolution of the monasteries and relics (rings at St Albans and an orb at Canterbury). The problem with all these is that the provenance is dodgy. The tomb has gone, as have all the rest and we are reliant on what amounts to the hearsay of chronicler-monks, who maintained these items at some point in the past.

If he was not the English knight he claims to be, perhaps he was Joannes ad Barbaum (Jean de Bourgogne) who died in 1372. We know the man wrote various medical books but the links with 'Mandeville' are thin. A third possibility is Jean d'Outremeuse, dying in 1400 at the age of seventy-two. Outremeuse lived in Liege although his surname too is suspicious – Outremer was the Medieval word for the Holy Land (literally, across the sea) which is a little too pat for someone writing about ocean-going voyages. 'Mandeville' might even have been Jean de Langhe from Ypres, a monk who wrote a number of treatises on other topics.

We can date Mandeville's manuscript to between 1351 and the mid-1360s, from various references in it. He himself claimed that he travelled the world for a non-stop thirty-four years and wrote the book in 1366. The first dated manuscript version is 1371, in Paris. It went into print for the first time (in Dutch) almost exactly a century later. A German edition, with illustrations, followed in 1478 and by 1515, when the Portuguese were making serious exploratory visits to east Africa, it had appeared in eight languages. Today, an astonishing 300 manuscripts of the handwritten version still survive, proving what a runaway best seller the book was.

Who read Mandeville? It was available in England, France and the Low Countries and we know aristocratic individuals who owned copies. Charles V 'the Wise' of France had one; so did that inveterate bibliophile Jean, Duc de Berri. Jean 'the Fearless', Duke of Burgundy, owned one, as did Thomas of Gloucester, Edward III's son. In both the *Knight's Tale* and the *Squire's Tale* in Chaucer's *Canterbury Tales* of the 1380s, there are references to Mandeville's travels. Perhaps to give the book some gravitas, it was translated into Latin. Some readers would have used Mandeville as a gazetteer. The first half of the book deals with various routes to Jerusalem, as the holiest shrine of them all and, rather like the Muslims and Mecca, Christians were expected to visit it once in a lifetime if they possibly could. It seems likely that 'Mandeville' himself was one such pilgrim, especially as his description of Jerusalem itself is fairly accurate.

But if the author of Mandeville actually went to Jerusalem, he certainly did not visit many of the other places referred to in the text. Anthony Bale, in the Introduction to his translation (*Oxford World Classics* series) is as kind as it is possible to be, when he describes the account as 'playfully unreliable'. More critical observers would say it is unadulterated nonsense, but there is no reason to suppose that many – or any – readers at the time saw it that way. Mandeville's was a generation brought up to believe every word of the Bible, for example, with no room for doubt. It was still the 'age of miracles', so Moses' parting of the Red Sea, Christ rising from the dead and the kingdom of Prester John were all part of the same marvellous reality.

If the author did not actually spend thirty-four years of his life travelling in mysterious places, where did he get his information from? His description of routes to the Holy Land (apart from the one he himself *may* have undertaken) came from William of Boldensele's *Liber de quilsusdam ultramarinius partibus* (the Book of Certain Overseas Regions) written about 1336. Another potential source is Odoric of Pardenone's *Relatio* (the Account) from around 1330. Odoric really *had* been to foreign parts, most notably to Russia and Asia, as a Franciscan missionary. It is probably from him that 'Mandeville' took his account of Prester John.

The mystical king appears in the second half of the book. In the modern Bale translation, this is on page 80 of a work that begins at page 5; but before we look at Mandeville's account, we need to evaluate Abyssinia in the narrative. We have to add the likelihood that Vasco da Gama or at least *someone* at the Portuguese court is likely to have read Mandeville or at least were aware of even earlier accounts. This explains why Abyssinia became associated with the Prester in the first place.

In the Bale translation, the country is called Ethiopia which is the more common ancient and medieval name for the land. According to the New Testament, on his way to Calvary, Christ collapsed and 'a man from Ethiopia' took up the cross for part of the journey. Mandeville says, 'The people in the south of this country are utterly black. In the south is a spring from which, during the day, the water is so cold that nobody can drink it, whilst at night, it is so hot that nobody can bear to touch it.' In essence, then, the water is useless to man, but we are immediately immersed into Mandeville's nonsense world, where everything is topsy-turvy. He offers no 'geological' explanation for this, but adds that the rivers have water that is 'murky and a bit salty, because of the intense heat'. Here we have a touch of reality; virtually every European to visit Abyssinia was struck by the extremes of temperature. It gets even more realistic however – the locals 'often have dysentery and don't live long', but this is immediately qualified by the 'fact' that they 'get drunk easily and have little appetite for food'. And then it becomes just plain silly:

> 'In Ethiopia, there are people who have only one foot and they get about so quickly on it that it's a wonder to behold; it's a large foot, which can provide shade and cover the entire body from the sun.'

This description comes from Pliny (Gaius Plinius Secundus the elder) who wrote a monumental thirty-seven volume *Natural History* in the first century AD. Having noted that, there is a fascinating echo of the sun-shade in the totemic umbrellas carried in ceremonies by, for example, Lemba Dengel.

'Also in Ethiopia,' Mandeville goes on, 'is the city of Saba and one of the three kings who made an offering to Our Lord at Bethlehem reigned there.' Saba may be the Biblical Sheba (although that was probably in what is today the Yemen) with the Old Testament links with Solomon and his mines. The connection between Prester John and the kings, the three magi or wise men will be discussed later.

What is altogether missing from Mandeville's very brief account of Ethiopia is any mention of Prester John. That is because Mandeville believed, as did virtually all Europeans who had heard the name, that the Prester was really king of India, not an African state. Despite all that we have discussed so far, it was the fifteenth century Portuguese who made the African connection and they got it wrong.

In Mandeville's day, 'the land of India' was divided into three. 'Greater India, an exceedingly hot region; Lesser India, a temperate region; and a third, to the north.' The fact that Mandeville is so vague about these, especially the north, not only exposes his lack of actual knowledge, but explains the confusion that swirled around 'the Indies' for centuries. As we shall see, there was a tendency in early European cartographers to assume that lands far away and unexplained were a series of islands rather than land masses. California was assumed to be separate from the North American mainland (which it might be one day, if the San Andreas fault cracks!). Africa below the Equator was also a series of islands. Because of the European obsession to obtain spices, largely as a food preserver, the Spice Islands (today the Moluccas in Indonesia) took on an importance far above their actual station in history. Because Christopher Columbus (Cristoforo Colon) believed he had discovered 'the Indies', the island he called Hispaniola in 1492, the term 'West Indies' was coined and stuck; the 'East Indies' made a little more sense, but only just.

It would be a brave man who would attempt to define the frontiers of Prester John's Indies (Mandeville avoids it) but, using the rivers and settlements referred to by him, we can make an educated guess. It covered the whole of modern India and Pakistan, including Sri Lanka to the south. It spread north-east to include the Ganges and most of what is today Tibet. In the north, it ran beyond the Indus to the region Mandeville calls Bactria, which for most of the twentieth century was in the USSR and is today modern-day Afghanistan, Tajikistan and Uzbekistan. In the west, it included much of Persia (today's Iran and Iraq), Southern Arabia and included part at least of Abyssinia and the horn of Africa. Such a huge empire – an estimated 7.5 million square miles in extent – would have accommodated umpteen tribes and peoples with a multiplicity of languages and faiths not seen again until the very different British Empire in the nineteenth century. In rough geographical terms, Prester John's kingdom was about 3,000 miles east to west and 2,500 north to south. The only other potentate to rival him was the Great Khan of Cathay (China) on whom Mandeville spends as many pages as on Prester John – and that, too, is a clue to the possible identity of the real man.

In geographical terms, Mandeville is all over the place. His written style is as didactic as it is engaging; there is no need for discussion – he is right. 'You should know,' he says, 'that the region of Prester John, Emperor of India, is underneath us [England or France, depending on one's view of authorship] for one travelling from Scotland or England towards Jerusalem keeps climbing'. Even to a man who believed the earth was round (see below) Mandeville was in no doubt that Jerusalem was the 'top' of it. Calvary, the hill outside the city where Christ was crucified, is at the very pinnacle. There is no concept of poles, North or South, in Mandeville.

On the very next page, after throwing us the Jerusalem 'googly', we have a flash of reality. Mandeville tells us that he heard a story when he was young (perhaps in the 1320s) about a 'courageous' man who left England, passed India and 'more than five thousand islands beyond' until he came to a land 'where he heard people speaking his own language and herding cows using exactly the same words as did people in his own country'. The courageous man had come home because by sailing east around a sphere, he had finally gone west! This was a bold statement to make in an age when all European universities taught that the world was a disc from the edge of which a traveller might fall. It was also two hundred years before Fernão de Magalhães (Ferdinand Magellan) proved that Mandeville's boyhood memories were correct!

Mandeville believed that Prester John's kingdom was made up of a series of islands, which may have been one way to explain the diversity of people and customs, rather as Madagascar has a very different biodiversity from southern Africa across the Straits. Prester John's main island was called Pentoxoire and his capital was Nisa. This may be Nishapur in today's Turkmenistan. It was referred to by various Greek writers up to the conquests of Alexander the Great in the 320s BC. China was richer and the Great Khan there more powerful but virtually all Prester John's trade was carried out with the east rather than the west, which was remote and probably explained why, to Europeans, the Prester was such a vague, almost surreal figure. Part of the trading problem was the dangerous waters around Prester John's coast (presumably India itself) because of adamantine rocks which acted as powerful magnets and ripped iron rivets from the hulls of sailing ships. Mandeville claimed to have seen whole artificial islands created from the wrecks of such ships. Traders travelling overland from Persia had an easier time of it, passing through Hormuz across the Straits from Arabia and reached Soboth where all their mercantile requirements were met, except wheat and barley (the locals ate rice, millet, cheese and fruit instead). There were parrots all over the place, like larks at home.

'The Emperor Prester John always marries the Great Khan's daughter and the Great Khan marries his.' In this single sentence, Mandeville gives us a clue to a possible reality of the situation. The implication is that the Prester was not a single individual, but a title, rather like Caesar given to the emperors of Rome, whichever family they came from. This in turn morphed into Tsar in Russia and Kaiser in Germany. So Mandeville seems to have believed that the rulers of these lands always married the Khan's daughter and this habitually happened with each generation. Allowing for the inbreeding problem, of which the fourteenth century was unaware, this was how Medieval alliances worked; countries made links through the intermarriage of their royal families.

Prester John was a Christian, Mandeville tells us and this explains his importance and his relevance to Europeans. His empire (kingdom is too small a word) lay sandwiched between enclaves of Islam; we shall examine the significance of this later. Most of his subjects were Christian too, but did not share the European articles of faith. They were very devout, however, and believed in the Trinity of Father, Son and Holy Ghost. They were loyal to each other and not greedy, setting no store by material possessions. Nowhere does Mandeville mention the unique churches carved from solid rock which we know were already in existence by his day; that was because he went nowhere near Abyssinia or any other part of the Prester's vast empire.

What interested Mandeville most and most of his readers, was the natural wonders which existed and were so different from the mundane flora and fauna of Europe. There was a sea in the empire made entirely of sand. Despite the lack of water, it ebbed, flowed and had waves just like any other sea. Locals were unable to cross it and so were oblivious of what lay on the other side. This may be the result of garbled reports of either the Thar Desert in modern Pakistan, or the Gobi, north of China. The lack of water did not prevent a good steady diet of fish, however. The animals were sweet to taste and had different shapes from the European types.

The most tantalizing reference concerned the huge mountain range from which a great torrent flowed which brought precious stones from paradise. The torrent was of sand, carrying with it huge boulders for three days every week, which disappeared into the sand of the sea. This made travelling there dangerous. Beyond the torrent was a plain with fruit trees that ripened every day at summer until midday when the trees shrivelled. Interestingly, Mandeville's explanation of this was that 'nobody does eat this fruit because it's a kind of magical illusion'. He neglects to say that this applied to nearly everything else in the lands of Prester John!

The locals in the plain/desert area were wild and 'utterly hideous' with horns on their heads. They grunted like pigs in lieu of human speech. The parrots, however, spoke as men do (Mandeville does not specify the language). Some had five toes, others three, the five-toed species much more vocal than the rest. The local name for these birds, Mandeville says, was pistake, a variant of the Latin *Psittacus* (parrot). Modern readers might have an altogether different explanation of the word!

Most of the fabled lands that Mandeville wrote about were crawling with precious stones. They were, and are, associated with extreme wealth and royalty, the decoration of crowns, orbs and sceptres, as well as noble tombs and shrines scattered throughout Europe and the Middle East.

The discovery of the diamond deposits at Kimberley (Colesberg Kopje) in 1866 was equated with the legendary King Solomon's Mines for years, at least in popular imagination. Prester John's stones included rubies, diamonds, sapphires, topaz, emeralds, chrysolites and irachite, the last being an unknown gem used to shoo away flies, always a problem in hot countries. Mandeville describes the entourage of Prester John going into battle, huge quantities of these stones in evidence, as well as gold, to show 'his lordship and power'. In front of the Prester, three gold, jewel-encrusted crosses were carried, each one defended by 1,000 men-at-arms (mounted knights) and 100,000 footsoldiers. On non-military outings, a plain wooden cross was carried in memory of the crucifixion and a golden bowl full of earth 'signifying that [the Prester's] nobility and his power shall become nothing and his flesh will return to the earth'. It may seem foolhardy in the extreme to flaunt all this wealth on a military campaign, but it was standard practice for European kings to take at least part of the royal treasury with them, both for incidental expenses and safekeeping. The tradition of carrying regimental silver plate for mess dinners was continued in the British army well into the nineteenth century.

Prester John's court was at his palace in Shush, Susa in modern Iran. The place was an ancient Persian capital and was destroyed by the Mongols in the thirteenth century. Some of Mandeville's description comes from *The Romance of Alexander*, a constantly changing, almost supernatural account of the great Macedonian general which prefigured epic poems of King Arthur and Charlemagne. 'The palace,' said Mandeville, 'is so magnificent that it's a wonder to describe.' Two towers had gold finials, set with gemstones so large that they operated almost as lighthouses after dark. The gates were made of sardonyx, a red and white stone associated with chastity. All the windows were made of crystal and the tables were of emerald, amethyst and gold. The steps that led to the Prester's throne were made from green jasper, cornelian, amethyst and calque. His footstool was of chrysolite, edged, as were the steps, with pearls and gold.

In the presence chamber, the roof supported by gold, gem-encrusted pillars, were twelve crystal vessels full of balsam to give off fragrance and 'to take away foul air'. The Prester's bed was gold studded with sapphires 'so that he may sleep well and refrain from debauchery, for he does not like to sleep with his wives except at four times each year according to the four seasons, and then that is only to conceive children.'

The court bristled with 30,000 courtiers every day, excluding visitors. The governmental structure was that Prester John was an overlord, rather as Agamemnon was in Homer's Greece. There were many minor kings under him and seven of them were present at the court at all times, each one rotating and serving for a month. Each king had seventy-two dukes, thirty earls and many more knights, Mandeville using the titles of nobility from France and England. Some of these courtiers were churchmen – the patriarch of St Thomas regarded with the same awe as the pope. This is clearly a nod to the Byzantine Greek Orthodox church, which had split from Rome centuries earlier and would survive, at loggerheads with the western papacy until Constantinople's destruction by the Muslims in 1453. There is, however, more to it than that, as we shall see later.

It took four months to cross Pentoxoire and beyond it was another island, Milstorak. The under-king here was Catalonabes, who created an estate on a mountaintop with fountains of wine, milk and honey. The place was crawling with beautiful virgins, mostly under fifteen and he called it Paradise. To Mandeville, Catalonabes was a Christian, but it is likely that this is a distorted version of Hassan I Sabbah, the leader of the Muslim Assassin cult known to us as the old man of the mountain.

Near Milstorak was the River Phison (the Ganges) 'that runs through India. There are many precious gems in that river, plenty of wood from the tree called *lignum aloes* and much gold sand'. On the left bank was the Valley of Devils, filled with sudden storms and terrifying noises of kettledrums and horns. This was the entrance to Hell, with a hideous devil's face carved in the rock that spewed fire.

Devout Christians were safe there, but those of shaky faith never returned. The noise of drums is probably a folk-memory of the Almoravides from Africa who invaded Spain in the late eleventh century. Rather like the Scottish bagpipes in another era, the drums were designed to terrify opponents on the battlefield. When Rodrigo Diaz, the Cid Campeador, halted the Almoravide advance at Valencia, he hung the captured drums on Christian altars to prove to the various congregations that they were just musical instruments, nothing more. The devil's face would have been familiar to Mandeville's readers through the mystery or miracle plays performed regularly at places like York and Coventry; 'Hellmouth' was a routine way to enter and exit the stage.

Mandeville went into the Valley of Devils with thirteen companions, including two Italian Franciscan friars. Only ten of them came out. There were precious gems everywhere 'whether or not it was exactly as it seemed I'm not sure, because I didn't touch them, because devils are so clever and cunning that they often make things seem to be something that they're not, in order to beguile people.' Mandeville also saw hundreds of Christian corpses, as though he and his friends had stumbled onto a battlefield. The force of the wind threw him to the ground, but God saw them (well, *most* of them) through it all. The bizarre combination of sensory perception and sights real or imagined, is either the work of pure fiction or a description of a drug-induced trip. The group who famously used hallucinogens in this period were, again, the Assassins.

The islands of Prester John continued. On one, the people were seventy feet tall and the sheep (which Mandeville saw often) the size of oxen. Yet another island was full of 'sinful and malevolent women, who have precious gems in their eyes. They have a way of looking at a man in anger and slaying him with their sight, as does the basilisk'. This creature, the gorgon of Greek mythology, had found its way into the Medieval Bestiary by Mandeville's day, a compendium of fictional animals that most people accepted as fact. But the notion of sinful women is a much wider concept. With the noted exception of Mary, Christ's mother, women were regarded as the weak link by Medieval man. They held nothing like the same status, in politics, religion or business and, because Eve fell for the Serpent's guile, were believed to have caused the fall of man from God's grace. They were liars and temptresses, the provocative gaps in expensive gowns in Mandeville's day known as the windows of Hell. The first genuine book which preached the evils of witchcraft, *Malleus Maleficarum* (the hammer of the witches), presented to Pope Innocent VIII in 1484, is one long misogynistic diatribe.

A sociologist/psychologist would have had a field day with Mandeville's next two islands. On the first were 'gadlibriens' (a corruption of Middle English for fools) whose sole job it was to take a new bride's virginity on her wedding night. They were regarded as idiots because taking said virginity was a dangerous thing and few new grooms would entertain the idea! This was because, according to the people to whom Mandeville spoke, wives often had serpents inside their bodies which bit the groom's penis during intercourse! The common appearance of blood from the vaginas of virgins caused by ruptured hymens is the biological explanation. Whether Mandeville's account is some half-baked version of the allegedly once-common European *droit de seigneur*, the local lord's right to take the virginity of one of his people, is unknown.

The next island was full of women whose emotions were upside-down. They were sad at the birth of their children and rejoiced if they died, burning them in mass funeral pyres. Husbands, already dead from natural causes, were then thrown onto the fire too. This has overtones of the Hindu practice of *suti* which the British outlawed in India in the nineteenth century, whereby widows were expected to die in the pyre that burned their dead husbands. Prester John's people explained the reasoning behind their attitudes; that being born caused sadness because children were facing a world of work and pain. Their deaths would take them to Paradise.

This was the island where some kind of democracy operated. Kings were elected for their morality and strength of character, not simply because they were the scions of wealthy, powerful families. They dispensed justice fairly and could not condemn a man to death without the consent of the aristocracy. If the king himself should commit a crime, he could not be executed, but was simply ignored by society until he starved to death. What we have here is a mish-mash of European culture. The idea of isolation may be the punishment of exile, which the Vikings, for example, used as the harshest penalty of all; loss of land, family and friends was far worse than maiming or death. The king's power circumscribed by the barons is, of course, pure Magna Carta. That document, sealed by King John at Runnymede in 1215, is one of the most over-rated documents in history. Today it is regarded, especially by Americans, as almost a blueprint for democracy. In reality, it was a list of sixty-three gripes by a greedy and self-interested barony who resented the king trying to rein them in. Not only did John personally tear up Magna Carta, it was officially condemned by Pope Innocent III and both king and barons proceeded to ignore it for centuries.

Interestingly, the next island that Mandeville considers *may* be Abyssinia. The locals here did not eat hares, poultry or geese, although all other animals and their milk were perfectly acceptable. There were communes here, in which children were raised by the entire group so that there were no issues of patrimony to contend with.

In terms of natural history, Mandeville lists the fauna, as usual ignoring flora almost completely. The crocodiles were actually snakes that swallowed men whole but had no tongues. They lived in the water at night and on rocks during the day and did not eat at all during the winter. In Arabia were 'girsants', a 'pretty animal, higher than a large horse and its neck is nearly twenty shaftments long. Its tail and rump are like those of a hart [deer] and it can see over a high house'. A 'shaftment' was a handspan from thumb to little finger, usually about six inches; the animal described was clearly a giraffe. Chameleons were everywhere, changing colour, except red or white and they neither ate nor drank. The pigs were spotted like fawns (peccaries), the lions were white and there were other beasts called 'longborans' or 'tontes' with black heads and horns 'sharp as a sword' with which they killed elephants.

The next island was full of goodie-two-shoes people. They were not Christian, but avoided all vice and were not jealous, greedy, lecherous or gluttonous. They followed broadly the ten commandments and placed no value on earthly possessions. This was the Land of Faith or the Island of Brahmins, the latter, of course, the name of one of the castes of Hindu India. Because of the locals' goodness, there was no crime, no war, no hunger; even the weather behaved itself. So impressive were these people that when Alexander the Great came eastward in the 320s BC during his campaigns across Persia towards India, he left them alone rather than invading them.

Alexander was linked to the next island, too. Here, the locals had feathers all over their bodies, except hands and faces and they could walk on water. They ate (like the Abyssinians) raw meat. Beyond the River Renemare, that bisected the land, were the oracular trees of the sun and moon, which predicted Alexander's untimely death in Babylon at the age of thirty-two. The wildlife in the region prevented Mandeville from going there – dragons, snakes, blue and white elephants, unicorns and lions.

In the island called Pytan were a small race ('but not as small as Pygmies' Mandeville tells us) who did not eat but who lived on the scent of wild apples.

At this point, Mandeville's description of Prester John's islands ends as if he has run out of imaginative steam. They would be 'too laborious to describe'. A page later, he begins the geographical narrative again. Orelle was made of pure gold mined by ants the size of dogs. Getting the gold from these canine insects was very difficult as they tended to kill human thieves. Argete was the silver island and the only star that could be seen from it was Canopus, the brightest in the southern constellation. Both these islands feature regularly in Greek mythology, the silver version becoming linked in the sixteenth century with Argentina in South America and the 'mountain of silver' at Potosi.

Tabrobane (Sri Lanka) also had a king chosen by election. It also had two winters and two summers, so that there were two harvests a year and the gardens bloomed all year round. It was home to many rich Christians.

The last area that Mandeville describes − or rather, cannot 'because I haven't been there' is Paradise. It is clear that this is not the same region mentioned earlier, but it is the highest place on earth 'so high that it nearly touches the sphere of the moon' and stood above the flood waters in the Noah's Ark story in the Old Testament. A wall surrounded Paradise and no one could tell what it was made from. In the centre was a spring that flowed into four rivers: the Phison (Ganges); the Gehon (Nile); the Tigris and the Euphrates. The Phison was still in some stretches, torrential in others and it was alternately hot and cold. The Gehon was always turbulent (perhaps referring to the cataracts along its route). The Tigris was so called because, like a tiger, it runs fast and the Euphrates meant 'growing well', describing its verdant banks.

Access to Paradise by humans was virtually impossible. Mountains and dangerous wildlife blocked the land routes; deadly seas destroyed ships. Those who had tried were exhausted by morning or made blind and deaf because of the roar of the waters. 'Whoever can proceed on this route,' wrote Mandeville, 'through the grace of God might arrive back at the same country they came from and so circumnavigate the earth ...'

One hundred and ninety years later, Ferdinand Magellan did just that.

'Here ends John Mandeville' is how *The Book of Marvels* comes to a sudden full stop. In it, we have the islands of the Prester, his court structure, the fabulous jewels of his throne room and his bed. What we do not have is the man himself.

So, where is Prester John?

Richard Denham

CHAPTER SIX: MARCO

POLO'S MISTAKE

John Mandeville devotes nearly as much of his book to the Great Khan as he does to Prester John, claiming that the Khan was more powerful and his empire larger. His lands were called Cathay, today's China, and to reach them, merchants had to travel through Pygmieland, whose inhabitants gave orders to normally-sized people, got married at six months old and rarely lived beyond the age of eight!

Correctly, Mandeville tells us that merchants from Genoa, Venice and Rome bought spices in Cathay. He is less accurate about the distances involved, claiming that it took eleven months to get there from any European port. There were thousands of wealthy cities in Cathay, but the largest, in the north, was Zanadu (Shang-du), made famous in England four centuries later by Samuel Taylor Coleridge in his Romantic poem, *Kublai Khan*. The city in the south, which eclipsed even Zanadu, was Cadom, today's Beijing, which was the Khan's capital.

As with Prester John, much of Mandeville's description of the Khan's court here is full of precious stones and beautiful decoration. Only silver is missing, because silver was regarded as rather common by the locals. There was a strict hierarchy in terms of seating arrangements in the throne room, the Khan himself towering over everybody else. The wives too (Mandeville mentions four of them) were arranged in order of precedence, the daughter of Prester John at their head. The feasts, four of them held every year on the occasion of the Khan's birthday, his circumcision, his first word and the first appearance of his miracles, were impossibly huge, lavish affairs involving thousands of people. The reference to circumcision is interesting, because it was not a European but a Jewish custom. Likewise, Mandeville explains the title Khan in relation to Ham, one of the three sons of Noah of the Old Testament, who ruled this part of the world after the Great Flood destroyed what had been there before. It is another reminder that in the fourteenth century, every word of the Bible, Old Testament as well as New, was taken literally. Every civilization on earth had developed from it.

The feasts were run by philosophers, who controlled the crowds in the hall as the Khan controlled his people at other times. They were experts in astronomy, necromancy, geometry and pyromancy, owners of dazzling scientific instruments like astrolabes (for navigation) and clocks. How much of this was a nod in the direction of the great philosopher K'ung Fu-tsu, whom the early Jesuit missionaries would call Confucius, is difficult to assess. European philosophy in Mandeville's day, based on ancient Greek via Roman texts, was largely mumbo-jumbo.

Minstrels played for the Khan and people bought him gifts. A keen huntsman, he owned many birds of prey and had elephants and baboons in his royal menagerie. His entourage when he travelled was huge. He rode in a vast chariot accompanied by legions of marching men. As he passed houses, the owners lit huge bonfires outside them and threw incense onto the flames to create sweet fumes for the Khan.

Mandeville is keen to mention local Christians were not molested. On the contrary, the Khan always doffed his hat – 'finely decorated with pearls and precious gems' of course! – in deference to their faith. They in turn carried crucifixes and holy water, singing *Veni avatar spiritus*, a common Pentecostal hymn in the fourteenth century.

The Khan's subjects took many wives, up to one hundred, and intermarried in their own families. Marriages were open, as in the lands of Prester John. They ate dogs, lions, rats and pretty much every animal except pigs, 'those beasts prohibited in the Old Testament'. They drank no alcohol, but relied on asses' and mares' milk.

Mandeville tells us that he and his travelling companions made a treaty with the Great Khan and his name was Kuyak. The real Guyuk Khan died in 1248, nearly a century before Mandeville wrote, which gives the lie to his supposed journey to the country. Equally spurious is the reference to a battle on the frozen River Ethel that stretches out of Cathay towards Prussia. This is the Volga, 'one of the greatest rivers in the world' and a hundred thousand men could fight on its frozen waters in the middle of winter. This is undoubtedly a reference to the 'battle on the ice' fought on Lake Prepius on the borders of Estonia, when the Russian hero Alexander Nevski destroyed the Teutonic knights' attack on his province in 1242.

Most of the references to Cathay and the Great Khan take us back to the previous century. John Mandeville never visited China; Marco Polo did.

At first glance, the *Divisament dou Monde* (Description of the World) usually called today *The Travels of Marco Polo*, look every bit as spurious as those of Mandeville. The difference is that Polo was a level-headed, hard-bitten Venetian merchant who travelled for business reasons and noted what he did with an eye to making money. In terms of reality, it is a pity that his co-writer (ghost writer may be a more accurate term) was Rustichello of Pisa, a romance writer who knew how to turn a humdrum travelogue into a best-seller. It is from him that most of the wilder stories emerge and quite possibly all the references to Prester John.

Polo was born into minor gentry in Venice about 1254 and when he was six, his father Niccolò and his uncle Maffeo set sail from Constantinople, the capital of Byzantium, for the port of Sudak in the Crimea. In the thirteenth century, Venice vied with Genoa and Pisa as the

Richard Denham

most dynamic business-oriented republics in Italy. Run by an official called the Doge and an elected council of businessmen, Venice was more like a modern corporation than a Medieval state. The fast, sturdy galleys that carried goods of all kinds, east and west, could be built in Venetian shipyards in a single day and no other Western state could remotely match them. Because of Venice's geographical location, trade with the Holy Land and further east was the norm. In fact, the Polo family had a permanent base in the Crimea, from which they traded with Turks and Russians.

From Sudak, the Polo brothers joined a caravan, literally a camel train that went east, partly along the banks of the Volga and partly by the river itself, to set up a trading base with Borka Khan, Lord of the Western Tartars. These nomadic peoples, fierce mounted warriors called Mongols today, were described with surprising accuracy by John Mandeville a century later. We shall discuss them in detail later because they are central to our search for Prester John. In 1260, the Polos were flying in the face of the advice of the papacy and westerners generally. *Tatarius* was the name of hell in classical mythology and the Christian church saw these horsemen of the Steppes as literally devils. The term 'tartar', in a much watered-down usage, was still current in Britain in the mid-twentieth century to mean trouble-maker.

The Polo trade mission went well, but they found themselves caught up in a tribal war in 1262 and lived at Bokhara until things quietened down, spending perhaps six years there, learning local languages and customs. All the evidence suggests that the Italians were welcomed and highly regarded, to the extent that they joined another trade embassy, this time to the court of Kubilai, the 'Great Khan' of whom Mandeville writes, who was Lord of Cathay with his palace at Khan-balik (Beijing).

Kubilai's reputation and status were immense and have largely remained so. He was a sophisticated philosopher, very different from the wild warriors who had carried out appalling slaughter all over Asia in the previous century and he expressed a particular interest in Christianity. Accordingly, he sent the Polos home to ask the

72

pope to send a hundred learned priests so that Kubilai could absorb their beliefs.

The timing was unfortunate. The pope, Clement IV, died during their return journey and squabbles between the papacy and the Holy Roman Emperor, which were a constant feature of Medieval realpolitik, meant that Peter's Chair was empty for three years. As luck would have it, Clement's eventual successor by 1271 was Tedaldo Visconti, Archdeacon of Liege. He was very open to the idea of a Christian mission run by Italians, and, as Gregory X, sent the Polos back to China with his blessing. The much-vaunted hundred-strong priest enclave never materialised. Only two went – Nicholas of Vicenza and William of Tripoli – and both died on the journey east. Someone who *did* get there, however, was Niccolò's son, Marco, now seventeen.

The Travels writes of Marco in the third person, which fits the idea of a ghost writer. Most scholars today assume that the book (which is actually incomplete and has a number of slightly differing versions) was written in 1298 when Polo and Rustichello were prisoners of war in Genoa. Who was responsible for the clear fabrications is uncertain, but since Rustichello had never been to China, some of it at least must come from Polo himself.

The man's personality is a blank canvas. His will, dated 9 January 1323, is a purely business document, with little in the way of sentiment. He left his estate equally to his three daughters and set free his Tartar slave, Peter. He was known by the nickname *Il Millione* (Million) which hints that he was all about money. Could his extraordinary travels have been that simple?

The Polos were well received again at the Great Khan's court and Marco learned four languages. Three of them were Mongol, Turkish and Persian, but the fourth is unknown. It may have been Mandarin Chinese. We have to be wary of Polo's claims. According to *The Travels*, the Khan sent him as an ambassador to nearby Kora-jang, which it took him six months to reach. The mission was, of course, a success, despite the fact that the lad was still a teenager and a foreigner entering a country where Europeans were like hens' teeth!

Polo stayed in the Khan's service for seventeen years and the account of his travels are essentially the wise and observant reports he brought back from Kubilai. As with the Portuguese who tried to leave Abyssinia three centuries later, the Polos were denied permission to go home because the Khan was so fond of them. Clearly, had the missions been genuine, there was ample opportunity for the Italians to slip away and head west whenever they felt like it. If only part of the adulation Kubilai showed them was true, of course, they probably preferred life in Beijing to the rough and tumble of strife-torn, permanently-sinking Venice.

'Now let me tell you the simple truth,' says *The Travels* and proceeds to hit the reader with an unlikely narrative of a sea voyage to India that took eighteen months! Of the 600 men who formed the crews of the 'four or five' ships, only 18 survived.

The Middle East section of *The Travels* covers factual sites that can easily be recognized – Armenia, Baghdad, Mosul, Tabriz and so on. Because this was Muslim territory, many of Polo's stories relate to miracles, both Muslim and Christian, which the writers accepted as true no matter how unlikely. Where possible, a Christian reference is given; for example, Saveh in Persia was the starting point of the Magi in their search for the boy king, Jesus Christ. It is Mandeville's Saba. They were buried in Saveh and Polo saw their perfectly preserved bodies (by now thirteen hundred years old) 'and they have hair and beards'. No one knew who these men were, apart from their names – Balthasar, Caspar and Melchior – and they were buried 'in days gone by'. This is particularly odd, because, as we shall see, their bodies were in Constantinople at the time. The whole of *The Travels* is a strange mix of legend and fact. Arab horses, which the Crusaders of the period knew well and used in desert warfare, are accurately described. Alongside that is Kala Atash-parastan, the town of fire-worshippers.

It is in the chapter called 'The Road to Cathay' that Polo mentions Prester John for the first time. While much of *The Travels* is basically accurate, with the usual mixture of guesswork and pure embellishment thrown in, *this* was the area where Polo made his mistake. He believed much of what he heard and what he heard was that north of the Mongol capital of Karakorum, on the barren Steppelands that were devoid of cities as the Italians knew them, lived a:

> 'lordless people ... actually tributary to a great Lord who was called in their language Ung Khan, which simply means Great Lord. This was that Prester John, of whose great empire all the world speaks.'

The Mongols' tribute amounted to one beast out of every ten. They were a nomadic people who followed their herds of sheep, cattle and horses and their population was growing. This bothered the Prester, so he adopted a policy of divide and conquer, intending to separate the tribes. The Mongol answer, like that of the Boers against British authoritarianism in the late nineteenth century, was to move north out of Prester John's reach and to avoid the tribute altogether.

The Polos visited Tenduc, north of the great wall and the Yellow River, across the Gobi desert – the 'dominion of Prester John'. Mandeville makes no such claims – his Prester, while an Asian emperor, was based on the three Indias and the Great Khan ruled Cathay. He has nothing to say about Mongolia to the north. The area in the Prester's time, Polo says, was ruled by the descendants of Prester John 'who is a Christian and a priest'. This particular Prester was George and, under the feudal system with which the Italians were familiar, he held the land as a vassal of the Great Khan. *The Travels* repeats the notion of intermarriage between the Prester's family and that of the Khan. The locals here lived by agriculture based on stock-breeding, but there was some commerce and industry (Polo does not specify what). Camel hair was sold and the area was rich in lapis lazuli for jewellery. Despite the Christian hierarchy, Tenduc was full of 'Mahometans' and 'idolators'. Islam had spread east from Arabia in the eighth century, just as it had spread west. The idolators were the Mongols, who had a faith of their own, and the term is not used with contempt as it usually was in Europe at that time. The Old Testament story of Moses' followers losing their faith in him and worshipping a golden calf was etched into the souls of European Christians. It was typical of the insular bigotry of Christians and Jews alike – *any* other form of worship was inferior to their own.

Even more confusing for the Polos were the Argons, 'half-breeds' of Muslims and idolators, who were more handsome and business-like than those of pure race. There seems to be an impossible blurring of understanding here. *The Travels* is talking of different religions, not races, so how can the 'half-breeds' have different racial characteristics?

Clearly, the Polos' Prester John was not the great overlord his descendants were. George was the sixth ruler with the Prester title and his provinces were divided into two; Gog and Magog. This has caused all kinds of confusion, especially in Britain, where the names are not references to places but to people. They feature in the Bible. Ezekiel 38 v. 2 says 'Gog, the land of Magog, the prince of Resh, Meschech and Tubal.' Gog, according to this version, was overthrown in a battle in the mountains of modern Israel. In the Mishnah, Gog and Magog were warriors who attacked the kingdom of God. The names may come from Gygos mentioned by the Greek historian Herodotus or Gugu, a name found in Assyrian inscriptions. Somehow, these names became linked with Britain, as in the prehistoric settlement in the Gogmagog hills near Cambridge. London was believed, for much of the Middle Ages, to be Troynovant, the new Troy, founded by Brutus, a survivor of the Trojan War and Gog and Magog were his warriors. For years, statues of the two were carried in mayoral processions in the City and copies of the eighteenth century carvings still stand in the Guildhall.

All this unnecessary complication is one of the many spin-offs from Prester John. As the Polos pointed out, Gog and Magog in the Tartar language became Ung and Mungul, the latter replacing 'Tartar' as the generic name for the tribes from the Steppes.

The Polos recount a story of Prester John and his dealings with the unnamed Golden King who ruled a neighbouring province. This was a folk tale, although precisely where it came from and who told it to the Italians is not recorded. The Golden King was rash enough to rebel against his overlord, Ung Khan (Prester John) and the Prester sent seven henchmen in disguise to offer their services to the Golden King. Playing the waiting game, these men remained in the King's service for two years, then they kidnapped him on a hunting expedition and took him back to Prester John. He was kept as a slave for two years, tending cattle and at the end of that, having learned his lesson, was returned with fine harness (armour) and a retinue of squires, to his own lands. The lesson? 'I know well,' the Golden King said, 'and have always known, that there is no man who can stand against you.'

What emerges from *The Travels* is a case of mistaken identity. To be fair to the Polos, it is not entirely their fault. Prester John was a character the European West believed in because, as we shall see in later chapters, they needed to. Neither were the Polos the only European visitors to the East in the middle of the thirteenth century. None of them was actually *looking* for him, unlike the Portuguese in Abyssinia, but they encountered his legend nonetheless.

Guillaume de Roubrouck was born in the French town of the same name about 1217. He was a devout friar, living in Paris as a young man and worked in some capacity for the equally devout Louis IX of France, who would be made a saint by 1297. One of the most accomplished of the French kings, Louis forced England's Henry III to relinquish claims to whole swathes of the French countryside and launched the sixth crusade in 1248. Like most of the others, this attempt to retake Jerusalem was a failure and after his capture by the Seljuks at Damietta, Louis returned home.

The crusading Christian spirit must have been in Louis's blood because he sent Roubrouck as a missionary in 1253 to baptize the idolators in the Mongolian steppes and perhaps form an alliance with them. Whether Louis had the earlier notion (see later) that somewhere beyond the reaches of Islam was a Christian king who would help the crusader cause, is unknown. Rather as various fictional agents in modern spy films are told that their maverick operations are not officially sanctioned by the government of the day, Roubrouck understood that what he was doing in no way made Louis IX a vassal of the Great Khan. The friar knew that there was a Christian sect – the Nestorians – in northern China and Mongolia and also knew that the Mongols, for all their terrifying military reputation, were surprisingly tolerant of other faiths.

Roubrouck left the crusader port of Acre early in the year with a party of other Franciscan priests and a Syrian guide, Omodeo. They travelled via Constantinople and the Black Sea and reached the camp of the Mongol leader, Sartaq. Rather as the Berbers of North Africa, the nomadic Mongols moved with their cattle herds and lived in padded, felt tents called *gers*, which became popular in the twentieth century as *yurts*. Sartaq was unsure what to do with these strange men with the peculiar language and passed the buck to Batu Khan, camped on the steppes three days' ride away. He in turn passed Roubrouck's people 'upstairs' to the court of Mongke Khan at Karakorum.

The friar was a keen observer of customs and behaviour and left the first truly detailed account of the Mongol way of life to reach the west. What he did not find were any of the monsters from the European bestiary and nothing to match the tall tales of sailors and merchants who had visited distant places. There were no cynocephali (dog-headed men) or the single-footed monopedes. Neither were there antipodes, men whose heels faced the front. No one had a face in the middle of his chest; there were not even any pygmies. Neither, if Roubrouck thought to ask, was there a Prester John.

Travelling across the steppes was hard and the poverty of the people apparent. Famine was commonplace and a lack of fuel (very few trees) meant that meat was often eaten raw, which may of course have been the source of any number of monster stories. The Great Khan was courteous, even friendly and Roubrouck often dined with him, but the Mongolian mindset was naturally suspicious and the Khan's people interrogated the Franciscans repeatedly. Nevertheless, Roubrouck was allowed to give his Christian sermons, apparently to a rapt audience. Exactly how this worked is unknown, because Onodeo the guide spoke none of the local languages! The Khan's mother, Sarghaghtani Beki was Christian, but she had also founded a Muslim college at Bokhara, so this was clearly a case, as with the much earlier Roman emperor Constantine, of a member of the ruling dynasty hedging their religious bets.

Mongke himself had a sophisticated, even modern, take on religion. As Roubrouck reported it, he said, 'We Mongols believe there is but one God, by whom we live and by whom we die and towards him we have an upright heart. But just as God gave different fingers to the hand, so has he given different ways to men.' At heart, however, most Mongols followed shamanism, burning bones to divine the future.

Roubrouck was unimpressed by Karakorum, not much bigger than St Denis, the village near Paris that he knew well. Even so, the place was surprisingly cosmopolitan, with quarters for clerics, builders and craftsmen, just like a European city. There was also a European colony, with merchants from Poland, France, Hungary and Germany; even an Englishman called Basil. This enclave was one of the best-kept secrets of the Middle Ages, because the produce they sold to the west was transported by middlemen and many – perhaps all – of them were probably presumed lost by their friends and families at home. Buddhism predominated in terms of religion, with twelve temples, but there were two Muslim mosques and a Christian (Nestorian) church.

The Franciscan seems to have blown his chances of conversion. He baptised six children and found one Nestorian convert (none from other faiths). He took part in scholarly debates on religion, but did not perform well and ended up threatening Mongke with hellfire and eternal damnation. The Khan seems to have been mildly amused by it all. Others would have buried the Franciscan and his party alive upside down in the ground, a traditional Mongol punishment.

Roubrouck came home disillusioned to report to Louis IX that the western Christian church was unlikely to make any headway in Mongolia. If anybody wondered if Mongke Khan was Prester John, wise and tolerant though he was, they were to be disappointed; he was not remotely Christian. And such is the lottery of the survival of historical records that Guillaume de Roubrouck's report was buried in the French archives, not to resurface until the nineteenth century, making Prester John and the whole Far East as elusive and mysterious as ever.

Almost nothing is known of a slightly earlier embassy to the Mongols, that of the English Dominican, David of Ashby. His account was written soon after 1260, so he may or may not have been sent east by Henry III, perhaps as a challenge to Louis of France, a race to reach the Far East. Only the chapter headings survive, with no accompanying detail, so we have to look earlier still, at the Italian Franciscan, Giovanni de Plano Carpini.

As we shall see in the next chapter, the wave of invasions by the Mongols was seen by the West as a miracle. There is a sort of parallel with the Second World War here. After Hitler's invasion of the USSR in Operation Barbarossa, Russia was an ally of Britain, Free France and the United States. This combination meant, in effect, that the Axis powers (Germany, Austria and Italy) could not win the war because they faced fighting on two fronts. This is how the west, especially the papacy, saw the Mongol hordes. According to the precept that the enemy of my enemy is my friend, the Mongols were seen as allies against Islam and for all the term Tartars, and their land, Tartary, was equated with the devil, perhaps it was the devil that they did not know which was preferable to Islam, the devil the Christians knew all too well.

It was this that lay behind Innocent IV's idea to send Carpini to the east, just as Louis IX was to send Roubrouck a few years later. Innocent was nothing if not ambitious. He wanted to unite the Greek and Roman Orthodox Churches with western Christianity in a common crusade against Islam – and had that been possible, it might just have worked. Both the Dominicans and the Franciscans were new religious orders in the mid-thirteenth century and, as friars, their main purpose in life was to preach. Their literal descendants, albeit of different denominations, were the missionaries who descended on 'darkest Africa' in the late nineteenth century.

Carpini's was the first of several missions to leave and he had no idea where he was going. Karakorum was unknown in the west and the Polos had yet to launch themselves on Cathay. He was himself overweight and in his sixties, hardly the stuff of which zealous missionaries are made, but he was a diplomat of the first order and had been a disciple of Francis of Assisi who had founded the order a few years earlier. At Easter time, 1245, Carpini left Lyons and travelled through Bohemia (today's Czechoslovakia), Silesia (now part of Germany) and Poland. At Breslau, he was joined by Friar Benedict who spoke various languages and would act as interpreter and guide.

The Mongols had overrun swathes of modern Russia by this time and Carpini's party was travelling through the extremes of winter to reach Kiev. The frozen ground was littered with bones picked clean by vultures and fortresses and villages lay burned to the ground. As they reached the camp of Batu Khan on the Volga, early in April 1246, they had to walk between two raging fires to purify themselves and then bow before a stuffed felt image of a god they did not recognize. They were amazed by the sumptuous interiors of the Khan's tents. If they were not *quite* as magnificent as Prester John's palace according to John Mandeville, they were still dazzling. The Khan sat with his wives and dignitaries and everybody ate from golden bowls; everybody except Carpini's people, because it was Lent and they only drank water and thin gruel. As he would do again eight years later with Roubrouck, Batu Khan sent the Franciscans on their way to the Great Khan at Karakorum.

The route was (probably deliberately) circuitous and exhausting. They covered 3,000 miles at thirty miles a day, usually in scorching heat, further east than any European had travelled. At this point, Carpini still believed in the dog-faced people and the Parossies, men who ate no food because of their tiny mouths; they ate by smell alone. And he almost certainly believed in Prester John, that either he or his descendants were to be found at their journey's end.

The Mongol prince Guyuk, whom Mandeville claimed was ruler while he was there nearly a century later, was crowned at the end of August in a massive four-day ceremony, witnessed not only by Carpini but by nobility and rulers from Russia, Tibet, China and even Egypt. The Franciscan noted that the colours of the court changed every day and the officer's horse harnesses were made of pure gold. There were furs, silk and jewels everywhere – much of it presents for the new Khan. The man was carried on a litter by four under-kings. Could he *be* Prester John? Carpini describes a strong, handsome, forty-something year old, but in fact he was in his twenties, his face and body ravaged by the alcohol to which he was addicted and which probably killed him just months later.

The go-between for the Franciscans was Chingai, the rough equivalent of chancellor or prime minister today (although western Europe did not have such a minister in the thirteenth century). The Great Khan played hard to get. He had already received the letters asking for support from Pope Clement and bridled at the fact that the emissaries had brought no presents, as was the custom.

Deprived of the chance to talk personally to the Khan or to convert his people to Christianity, Carpini spent his time describing in writing the customs he saw. The Mongols were shamanistic, deeply superstitious and they sacrificed their tough, short-legged ponies to a sky god called Tengri. With more hope than common sense, the Franciscan believed that the Chinese, as opposed to the Mongols, were more likely converts because they had saints, church-like buildings and an Old and New testament. None of this was true.

Eventually, Carpini was given an audience with Guyak Khan, but he found him even more dogmatic than the people he served and just as ready to use force to demand that the western papacy bow down before him. It was not the Mongols who destroyed armies and cities and burned villages, but Tengri, the eternal god. The language used, in a letter from Guyak that still survives in the Vatican Archives, is not dissimilar to the old western crusader battle cry *'Deus Io Vult'* – God Wills It.

But what, in all these bizarre travels, of earnest friars and successful merchants, of Prester John? Marco Polo believed that the man was real, that he had travelled in his empire and had traded with his merchants. The stuffed felt image that Carpini and, no doubt, Roubrouck, saw everywhere was not, as it turned out, a god, but Genghis Khan, known to the west as 'the Hammer of God'.

If this great warlord, the Mongols' 'perfect warrior' was not Prester John, then who was?

Richard Denham

CHAPTER SEVEN: THE

HAMMER OF GOD

Hollywood has made two films about Genghis Khan, both of them, in different ways, appalling. The first was *The Conqueror* in 1956 when a dreadfully miscast John Wayne stuck on a false moustache and rode at the head of a couple of hundred native Americans from the Navaho tribe as the scourge of Europe. The movie had tragic repercussions because filming took place in the Nevada desert where nuclear tests had been carried out; the resulting illness and even deaths of several cast and crew members left a nasty taste. *Genghis Khan* nine years later was little better, when Omar Sharif put the fake whiskers on and ran rings militarily around Chinese emperor Robert Morley. It was all highly unconvincing and another box office flop; at least Wayne admitted he had starred in a turkey. The biggest mistake was assuming that an American or an Egyptian could play a Mongolian who was also the best general of the Middle Ages, but it spoke volumes about the west's failure to understand Genghis Khan even after eight hundred years.

The problem, as with so many primitive peoples of the ancient world, is that the Mongols had no written language, so their entire history, up to Genghis' time and slightly beyond, was shrouded in myth and legend. His successor as Great Khan, his son Ogedai, commissioned an official work, the *Secret History of the Mongols*, written in the appropriated Uighur script and explaining the rise and greatness of his illustrious father. It traces Mongol heritage from the union of a blue wolf and fallow doe, which is precisely the same kind of creation myth we find in every people of the past, including the Old Testament. For the wolf and the deer, read Adam and Eve.

But, just as there are glimmers of fact in the Old Testament, backed by other, independent accounts and archaeology, so *some* of the *Secret History* rings true. The Far Eastern mainland in the twelfth century was a complex map of tribal territories with blurred frontiers and shared customs and practices. Nearest to Europe, south east of the Caspian and Aral Seas, was the Khwarazamian Empire, extending south to the Himalayas where John Mandeville believes Prester John reigned. To the east of that, between Lake Balkhash and the Takla Makan desert was the Kara Khitai Empire and the tribes of the Uighers, Namans and Kereyids further east still. North across the steppes towards Lake Baikal and the River Amur were the Merkids, the Mongols and the Tartars. Straightaway, we are in a world of confusion. To the Christian west, Mongols and Tartars were the same thing; in fact, anyone east of the Caspian was regarded as a Tartar. In the same way, Muslims referred to all Europeans as the infidel (unbelievers) irrespective of national origins. South of the Gobi desert were the Onguts and Tanguts and the empires that today form China – Hsi-Hsia, Chin and Sung. There is no mention of anywhere called Cathay, which was exclusively the European name for the area.

The boy who would become the hammer of God was born, probably in 1167, into the Bjorjin clan, a subdivision of the Mongols. He was named Temujin and the Tartars murdered his father when he was nine years old. Western Europe would have been appalled by the barbarity of the Mongols had they known about any of this, but similar betrayal, treachery and slaughter was being carried out in feudal Europe on a daily basis. Inter-tribal warfare was a way of life, as it had been, for example, in Britain before the arrival of the Romans and in North America before the arrival of white settlers. Temujin quickly learned the laws of survival, allying with one clan chieftain after another to defeat a common enemy. He rode with his blood brother Jamukha and with To'ori, leader of the Kereyids who were Nestorian Christians. It may be that working with him led to the future Khan's tolerance of alien religions.

Beyond the bickering and almost casual slaughter of the steppe tribes lay the Chin, the ancestors of modern China, who were sophisticated, literate and highly manipulative. They had invented gunpowder, paper and the printing press, technological advances that would remain unknown to Europe for years. They were also adept at absorbing minor outlying tribes, buying their military prowess and reducing the risk of war. Today's China is still carrying out this policy today, bullying Tibet and Hong Kong, extending its cheap technology wherever it can in the world; the additional overlay of Communism hardly matters in that respect.

Both Temujin and To'oril fought as mercenaries for the Chin and the Tartars were brought to heel as a result. To'oril became Ong Khan (Wang Khan in the Chin dialect) and it is possible that 'Ong' became transcribed in the exchange of languages to the 'John' of the Europeans. This explains Carpini's assertion that Prester John defeated Genghis Khan because the pair fell out in 1203 and Temujin's forces were indeed driven back to Lake Baljuna.

Before this split, Temujin tried to strengthen his own position as lord of the eastern steppes by marrying his eldest son Jochi to Ong Khan's daughter. This was one of several incidents that led to a deterioration of relationships between the two warlords; Ong Khan was furious at Temujin's effrontery. It is also of course the origin of the garbled story, reflected in Mandeville and Roubrouck, that Prester John always married the daughter of the Great Khan.

The death of Ong Khan meant that Temujin was able to make headway against the Kereyids who were first defeated, then, like Caesar before him and Napoleon after him, Temujin recruited them into his ever-growing army. Tolui, Temujin's youngest son, married Sorghaghtan Beki, Ong Khan's niece, adding further to the legend of Prester John's marital status.

The only tribe that still opposed Temujin were the Naimans and in the Year of the Rat (1204) he destroyed them with battlefield tactics that had not been seen before. At a quriltai, a summit meeting of tribal leaders, Temujin was declared master of all the steppe tribes and given the title Genghis Khan, the perfect warrior.

What was the secret of the new Khan's success? Luck must have played a part as it did in every general's career, but he must also have had terrific charisma to hold the loyalty of his people, now strung out across 3,000 miles of territory, east to west. In place of the old *anda* system of sworn brotherhood, which Genghis knew from bitter experience did not work, he set up a *nokar* system, similar to the feudalism of western Europe, whereby men pledged their support in exchange for bounty and position. Unlike most European rulers, he did not rely on nepotism, regarding his family with suspicion. He also created the *keshig*, a personal bodyguard of devoted warriors who grew from 150 men to 10,000 in the space of two years. The Romanovs in Russia, the emperors in ancient Rome and innumerable lesser fry all over Europe employed men in this way and as long as the *keshig* remained faithful to Genghis, which it did, he was almost untouchable. The problem could arise of the bodyguard becoming too powerful in their own right, like the Praetorians of ancient Rome and the often-raised question 'who guards the guards?' implied that this group was more powerful than the emperor himself. In the case of Genghis Khan, however, there appears to have been no insubordination.

But what really explained Genghis' meteoric rise and the power that he wielded was the brilliance of his army and this would become even more obvious when he took on the west. He introduced, 600 years before Revolutionary France and 700 before First World War Britain, conscription for all men over the age of fourteen. Priests, doctors and undertakers were the only ones exempt from service. The heart of the Mongol army was the cavalry, riding sturdy, short-legged ponies that look almost comical in modern re-enactments of Golden Horde armies. Mongols were born to the saddle, among the first to use what may have been another Chinese invention, the stirrup, to control their animals better and make their seats secure. It enabled the hard riders of the steppe to leave both hands free to hurl lances and fire bows in a way that, for example, the stirrupless Roman cavalry had been unable to do.

A recruit was encouraged to bring horses with him, perhaps as many as five and all of these would take part in a campaign, warriors leaping from one saddle to another to carry on a pursuit or a charge. Families joined too so that camp followers had an army of cooks, carriers and nurses as back-up. The camps, hundreds of gers loaded ready-built onto pack animals, were commanded by quartermasters called *justchis*, whose word was law. The army units, like the legions of Rome or the regiments of modern armies, were composed of ten, a hundred, a thousand and ultimately, ten thousand men.

Next to the skin, the Mongol warrior wore yet another Chinese invention, a silk shirt. Whereas silk remained expensive in western Europe – a whole industry was based on keeping the Silk Road open – it was cheap in the east. It was also highly practical; the barbed arrows of the mounted archers caused dreadful damage when they were pulled out of wounds – wrapped in silk as they were, driven into such a wound, lessened the damage and blood-loss considerably. Over the shirt, the Mongol horseman wore a long tunic of felt, the same thick wool from which the gers were made. Over that, a breast and backplate of overlapping leather and iron plates added to protection, with an iron or copper helmet that left the face free, rather like the headgear of most western foot-soldiers. Leather-covered wicker shields, lighter than the European version, could be slung over the back and every man carried a straight-bladed, two-edged sword, at least one lance (probably two) and a composite bow made from bamboo and yak horn. Each quiver contained sixty arrows and firing at speed from the saddle was an astonishing skill rarely, if ever, seen in the west.

The typical tactic of these fierce horsemen was to approach in a long line at a walk. As the pace increased, the men on the flanks moved forward to form a pincer movement, encircling an enemy not ready for this and bewildered by its speed.

It was this speed of attack, both on and off the battlefield, that gave the Mongols the edge. They had a signalling system, using flags and fast riders in the day, with flaming torches at night, to pass orders and intelligence between units. Although foot-soldiers were employed from time to time, no Mongol army had to wait for a lumbering baggage train or clutter itself with siege engines, at least not until they took on China itself.

Much of the terror generated by the Mongols was that they came out of nowhere and attacked small villages and hamlets. They were the eastern, mounted equivalent of the Vikings who raided the British coast with impunity in the eighth to ninth centuries. By the time the local Saxon thegn or even the king turned up, the Vikings had long gone, leaving ruined settlements and looted monasteries in their wake. The Mongols left cities alone because they had no siege weapons, like the towers, mangonels and trebuchets used across Europe. Just as the Vikings began with lightning raids that morphed into permanent settlement, so the Mongols developed their strategy too. In 1211, they crossed into Chin territory and routed a Chinese army who could not cope with their speed of attack. Although we should be wary of the numbers that various chroniclers throw about, it is possible that the Chin army numbered 70,000 men. They were routed in hours. Genghis Khan's eldest son, Jochi, reached the gates of Chung-Tu, the Chin capital that would become Beijing years later. Then he rode home, laden with booty.

This happened twice more and the slaughter increased each time. We have no accurate way of assessing this. Used as we are to deaths and casualties on an enormous scale in the wars of the twentieth and twenty-first centuries, we have to remember that the Mongols had nothing remotely to compare with the weapons of mass destruction of our own time. What makes the difference is that the Mongols recognized no laws of western chivalry, however selective these may have been. Neither did they have a Geneva convention to protect civilians, women and children. In fact, thousands of the latter were taken as slaves by the Mongols. The *Yasa*, the law system imposed by Genghis in 1206 demanded the death penalty for desertion, adultery, espionage, theft and bankruptcy; there is no mention of murder. It was a harsh way of life that few outsiders could live with.

In 1203 the third Mongol attack was on an unprecedented scale, three separate columns attacking three areas simultaneously; one moving east to Chung-Tu and the sea; one due south into Hsi-Hsia and the third across the Yellow River into the Sung Empire, the heart of China itself. When the invaders settled down for the siege of Chung-Tu, the emperor fled and the starving population resorted to cannibalism. The houses were burned down and thousands of residents were hacked down in the blazing streets. The ground was slippery with human fat.

The collapse of the capital led to a rapid panic over the whole country and the Chinese deserted to Genghis in droves. This was accepted with generosity by the Khan, on the understanding that it was honoured. A slow and ghastly death awaited anyone who broke his word.

It was now that Genghis Khan turned his attention to the west. Beyond the desert of Kizil Kum and the Hindu Kush mountains of the Indian frontier was the Khwarazmian Empire of the Shah. This, in the ancient world, was Persia, whose king, Darius, had been trounced by the much smaller force of Alexander the Great and his Macedonians. Just as the memory of Genghis Khan was to last for centuries in the east, so tales of Alexander survived across central Europe as far as the Indus. When the mercenary commander Georg Kastrioti fought for the Ottoman Turks in the fifteenth century, they called him Skander Bey, Lord Alexander, in honour of a man who had died eighteen hundred years earlier.

The Shah in Genghis' day was Ala al-Din, who led what was probably, in the early thirteenth century, the largest army in the world. His capital was Samarkand, still today a place of mysticism and fabulous wealth. It had perhaps half a million inhabitants, with shady streets, gardens and fountains. It sold melons and aubergines, packed in lead-lined boxes filled with snow for export. Cotton was grown and woven here; so was silk and its carpets and jewellery was legendary to the east and the west.

In 1216 Genghis sent ambassadors to the Shah with letters, that have survived. They were an offer of trade and friendship, but there was a veiled threat there too. Genghis referred to the Shah as his 'son', an impossibly patronizing reference. He also warned of his power – 'my country is an anthill of soldiers and a mine of silver'. He did not want more land, he said, but made it clear that he had the men and materiel to take it if he so chose. Since the letter's seal referred to Genghis as 'God in heaven; the power of God on earth, the emperor of mankind' there was little doubt that he saw himself as the senior partner in any future alliance.

It was only a matter of time before war broke out and in 1218, a wing of the Mongol army under the command of Subedei Bat'atur of the Reindeer People clashed with the Shah's son, the highly competent Jahal al-Din south of the Tien Shah mountain range. With four sons, all of whom were competent generals, Genghis could provide a powerful challenge to the greatest power on earth. His army was perhaps half that of the Shah's, but the speed of the Mongol attack caught the Muslims napping. Genghis crossed the Kizil Kum desert, which the Shah assumed was not possible and appeared 400 miles behind enemy lines. Bokhara, the 'cupola of Islam' according to one chronicler, was destroyed and Genghis marched into the principal mosque, tearing up the Koran with his own hands and lecturing the defeated imams from the pulpit. 'I am the punishment of God,' he told them. 'If you had not committed great sins, he would not have sent a punishment like me.' He ordered the mosque converted into stables for his cavalry. One estimate claims that 30,000 were killed in less than two days.

For the next three years, Genghis continued his hunt for the Shah and his family. His own upbringing had taught him that revenge was not only sweet, it was necessary for future peace. The early raids on China had seen the Chinese re-entering their abandoned villages and cities once the Mongols had gone. This was different; it was conquest and nothing would be the same again. His armies laid waste whole regions of what is today Afghanistan. Balkh, once a city to rival Samarkand where Alexander had dined and the philosopher Zoroaster had preached, was left an empty shell. It is still so today. The Shah, on the run and broken, died, probably of pleurisy on an island in the Caspian Sea in January 1221. For the first time in five years of continual campaigning, Genghis Khan went home.

'My descendants,' he wrote, when nearing death, 'will wear gold, they will eat the choicest meats, they will ride the finest horses, they will hold in their arms the most beautiful women and they will forget to whom they owe it all.' Eventually, that may have been so, but not for years to come. He died in August 1227 while the army was still fighting against the Tanguts. They hacked their way into the capital and, in memory of their beloved leader, slaughtered everything that moved, human or animal, inside the city.

Genghis Khan was buried in the Burkhan Kaldun mountains having lain in state for three months. Forty slave girls and forty horses were buried with him; he would need them all in the afterlife. Then his cavalry, who had made him what he was, rode over his grave and it disappeared without trace.

The West should have listened to Father Giovanni Carpini in the late 1240s. Genghis Khan had been dead for only twenty years. After him, his son Ogedei and *his* son Guyuk continued the line, although later Khans, like Khubilai and Mongke, were descended from Tolui, Genghis' youngest boy. Carpini saw images of the dead perfect warrior everywhere and he was able to assure everybody that he was not Prester John. It was just possible that Ong Khan was, but since Ong's power had been well and truly eclipsed by Genghis, this too was unlikely.

But nobody was listening to Carpini. His accounts,

by no means totally accurate, were read only by papal clerks and perhaps the pope himself. Unlike Mandeville, and even Polo, there was no runaway bestseller. Instead, Europe held its collective breath with another Prester John wannabe who called himself King David.

In 1220, while Genghis Khan was driving west and mopping up the scattered, demoralized armies of the Shah, reports began to appear in Christendom of an army invading Persia led by 'King David, Christian King of India, sent by the Lord to crush the heathen and destroy Mohammed's teaching'. These reports continued for three years. Clearly, 'King David' was Prester John and after Persia, his next target would be the Holy Land itself, over which the western Christians had all but lost control.

The king of Hungary sent a letter to the pope, Honorius III, in 1223 that, 'a certain King David, or as he is usually called, Prester John' was rampaging through Georgia and the Russian provinces north of the Black Sea, slaughtering thousands. This was, of course, Subedai Bat'atur and it must have been obvious, bearing in mind the new targets, that he was not Christian at all. It took twenty years for this message to be heard, and then, not by everybody. On Palm Sunday, 24 March 1241, the city of Cracow in modern Poland was burned to the ground. Today, in St Mary's Church in the main square, a trumpeter still blows the alarm from the tower, in memory of the original alarm sounded that Sunday long ago.

The attackers were the 'dog-faced Tartars', yet they were still equated by enlightened (and now confused) Europeans with King David. Worse, a Christian community had been attacked by the Christian king of India, Prester John.

CHAPTER EIGHT: A

PRESTER JOHN LETTER

The letter began 'John, priest by the almighty power of God and the might of our Lord Jesus Christ, King of Kings and Lord of Lords …'

It was written in Latin in 1165 and delivered to three of the most powerful leaders of the Christian world: the Pope, Alexander III; Frederick Barbarossa, the Holy Roman Emperor; and Manuel Comnenos, Emperor of Byzantium. Although it was a formal, official document, the one addressed to Comnenos, for example, referred to '[Prester John] friend, Emmanuel, prince of Constantinople, greeting, wishing him health, prosperity and the continuance of divine favour.'

The fact that these three men received the letter tells us a great deal about the state of religion and European politics in the mid-twelfth century and it explains why Prester John was so important to the west. Alexander III was the first of the lawyer popes. His name was Rolando Bandinelli from Siena and he issued more decretals (formal papal letters) than any other pope of the twelfth century, many of which concerned England. The reason for this was the complexity of European politics. This was a time of a schism or split in the western church, because although Alexander theoretically sat in Peter's Chair at the Vatican for over twenty years, he had a number of rivals at Avignon in the south of France. The first of these, Ottaviano de Monticelli, who called himself Pope Victor IV, tried to rip the scarlet cloak from Alexander's shoulders during his inauguration ceremony.

Although the 'real' Pope was not intimidated by the existence of his rivals, he had to tread warily with various European kings. One of the most aggressive, from Alexander's point of view, was Henry II, whose on-going feud with his Archbishop of Canterbury, Thomas Becket, was blowing up out of all proportion. Becket, from a relatively humble background, had been Henry's drinking buddy and Chancellor; they even shared mistresses. When the king appointed Becket to the See of Canterbury, however, all that changed. Becket got religion. He wore a penitent's hair shirt under his robes that chafed the skin continuously and had himself flogged by the monks of Canterbury to atone for his sins. He also backed his churchmen against Henry II's legal system and the issue of 'criminous clerks' reached Alexander's ears in Rome.

The problem was a perennial one in western Europe. Where should a man's loyalty lie? To the king, who technically owned the land he lived on? Or the pope, his spiritual father, who was God's lieutenant on earth? As long as Becket remained stubborn in defending his people and defying the king, Alexander was loath to interfere. His instincts, of course, were to support Becket, but that risked alienating Henry who might have thrown in his lot with the Holy Roman Emperor. Becket's murder, almost certainly on Henry II's orders, in 1170, eased the problem and Alexander brought Henry to book, forcing him to do penance by walking barefoot to Canterbury where Becket had been hacked to death and being flogged by the monks there.

The Holy Roman Empire came into existence on Christmas Day 800 when Charlemagne was crowned Emperor of the West by the pope of the day, Leo III. Technically, the first Holy Roman Emperor to use the title was Otto I in 962 and by that time, the tradition existed that the Emperor was always German. This tradition, of hereditary German princes 'elected' by underlings, continued throughout the Middle Ages. The problem here was simply a larger version of the squabble between Henry and Becket; who ruled, the emperor or the pope? It should have been a simple matter of demarcation – the emperor would preside over temporal matters; the pope over spiritual. But in practice, church and state went hand in glove, so such neat, clear-cut lines were impossible to draw. Consequently, it became an endless clash in an insoluble power-struggle, dependent largely on the personalities of individual popes and emperors.

After the fiasco over who should actually *be* pope in 1159 (Rolando won by a clear vote count among the cardinals) Alexander could not stay in Rome because of the power of his rivals' families. He was also, to an extent, at the mercy, as all popes were, of the Roman mob, who for centuries had been whipped up by ambitious politicians to go on the rampage. The Holy Roman Emperor threw in his lot with the antipope, Ottaviano (Victor IV) and Alexander excommunicated him.

Frederick I, the red-bearded, of the Hohenstaufen family, had been elected in 1152 on the death of his uncle. A strong and capable ruler, he put down various rebellions in his broad-based empire and deliberately set up a succession of antipopes after Victor, merely to spite Alexander.

In 1165, the year that the pope and the emperor received Prester John's letter, Alexander returned to Rome with the blessing of the Senate, no longer the powerful organization it had been in ancient Rome, but, in effect, a city council. Without a pope in the eternal city, the pilgrim trade was drying up and that meant a loss of money which went against the grain in cash-centred Italy. Frederick did his best to waylay Alexander, even hiring pirates to hit his ship in the Mediterranean (he had been in hiding in France) but the pope's sailors got away from them. The build-up of tension between pope and emperor never went away and it may explain why the Prester John letter was received with

such hope, at least by the papacy. Two years later,
Barbarossa led an army across the Alps, with its folkloric
memories of Hannibal and his elephants and marched on
Rome itself. On Whit Monday, 29 May 1167, the largely
German army smashed its way into first the city, then the
Vatican. The 'holiest shrine' in Europe had been desecrated
and even if the numbers of casualties were nothing by
Mongolian standards, the marble floors of St Peter's were
littered with corpses, including those of unarmed clerics and
the high altar was splashed with blood.

The third recipient of the Prester John letter,
Emanuel Comnenos, formed the third angle of the
Christian triangle that dominated Europe. In the endless
power struggle between politicians claiming to be emperor
of Rome (there were six such claimants in 306 alone)
Flavius Valerius Aurelius Constantinus emerged as
Constantine, subsequently called the Great. His mother was
a Christian and the new emperor embraced the faith
alongside the existing pantheon of Roman gods, probably as
a fail-safe precaution. He set up a new capital on the
Bosphorus which became Constantinople (Constantine's
city in Greek) and this in turn became the heart of the
Byzantine empire.

This split in the Roman empire may have been a
practical and pragmatic solution to the sheer size of it, but it
actually created a 'them and us' mentality which barbarians
from outside could exploit. Although both Constantinople
and Rome were Christian by the late fourth century, each
regarded the other as heretics and co-operation between the
two was rare. By the sixth century, Byzantium, famous for
its arcane and bizarre politics, had spread as far west as
Greece and Macedonia, the whole of modern Turkey and
the Middle East, including what would become the crusader
states, Egypt and a strip of coast in North Africa equating to
modern Libya.

The first of the Comneni family to rule as emperor
was Alexius I in 1081. Manuel, who took the throne in
1143, attempted with some success to add the Italian states
and Hungary to his empire with the usual Medieval mix of
diplomacy and war. He was less successful against the Turks

however, being defeated by them in battle in 1176. This is the key to the recipients of the Prester John letter – all of them, the pope and both emperors, were not merely Christian leaders; they were, by definition, enemies of Islam. So was Prester John.

The letter was extremely important, because here, at last, after years, perhaps centuries, of doubt and rumour, was tangible proof of the man's existence. The first paragraph thanked the three recipients for the 'objects of art' that they had sent him – of which there is scant record – and the fact that Prester John had commanded his treasurer to send his own presents in return (again, there is no record of anything having been received).

John knows that he is a distant and legendary being, so he outlines in the letter various facts about his empire, the text being lavishly furnished with dollops of self-praise – 'Excellency', 'Magnificence', 'Exaltedness' are everywhere; and the capital letters are important. Reading it today, we can immediately see where Roubrouck, Carpini and 'Mandeville' got their ideas from. The letter was circulated, copied and paraphrased into many languages and even today, over 100 manuscript copies still exist.

Prester John, the letter tells us, 'surpasses all under heaven in virtue, in riches and in power'. Bear in mind that he was writing to three men who possessed riches and power in abundance and, no doubt, all of them saw themselves as virtuous. Seventy-two kings paid tribute to Prester John and, contrary to the later beliefs of the Portuguese explorers and writers like John Buchan, 'in the three Indies our Magnificence rules'. But that was only the heart of his empire; it extended much further. Even so, there was no mention of Abyssinia or even Africa where the Portuguese later searched for him; nor of Mongolia where Genghis Khan would wreak havoc over half a century after the letter arrived. Prester John's empire, it claimed in 1165, 'extends beyond India where rests the body of the holy apostle Thomas; it reaches towards the sunrise over the wastes and it trends towards deserted Babylon near the Tower of Babel'. We shall look at the apostle Thomas later, but both Babylon and Babel were well known to Europeans from the Old Testament.

Babylon was an ancient city on the banks of the Euphrates, not far from the earthly paradise of the Garden of Eden from which Adam and Eve had been expelled for breaking God's laws. It had once been a vast, sprawling settlement, the headquarters of Hammurabi and Nebuchadnezzar, with temples and ziggurats soaring into the sky. The Assyrian king Sennacherib destroyed it in the seventh century BC and despite rebuilding, it was once again a ruin when the Roman emperor Trajan visited it in 115AD.

Babel was altogether more conjectural. According to Genesis 2, it was a tower built by Noah's descendants after their survival of the Flood and one intended to reach heaven. God found this arrogant and offensive and hit the builders with a plethora of different languages and scattered them all over the earth, explaining the origin of various races. The building collapsed. Several ziggurats and other towers in what was Babylonia (present-day Iran) have been suggested by archaeologists as the original Babel, but, almost by definition, hard evidence is lacking.

The fauna described by Prester John is an interesting mix of the now-banal and purely fantastic, but we have to remember that wild species were largely a mystery to Europeans brought up without television and David Attenborough! Elephants came as little surprise. The Romans knew of them, were attacked by them under Hannibal and Nero even used them to pull chariots! Herodotus and Strabo, wannabe historian and geographer respectively, both describe them. Even so, they were a novelty. The first recorded elephant in England, for example, was a gift from Louis IX of France to Henry III, landing at 'Wythsand' (probably Sandwich in Kent) in the autumn of 1255, accompanied by his keeper, Henricus de Flor. The chronicler Matthew Paris made a realistic drawing of it, but his camels, by comparison, are hopeless; he had never seen one. Prester John had; his empire teemed with them, but his letter uses the term as opposed to dromedaries, so presumably the camels are Bactrians. Both breeds were used extensively as beasts of burden all over what had been Persia, the Middle East and the Far East and merchants following the spice or silk roads would have been very familiar with them. Crocodiles too were familiar to anyone along the Nile, though the first recorded mention of them in England does not occur until the reign of James I, when there were several in the Paris Gardens, alongside Bankside, a disreputable 'stew' full of brothels, bear-pits and theatres. Wild horses are the nearest we come in Prester John's letter to the rugged ponies of the steppes and wild asses are included in the menagerie. These animals were hardly exotic; various breeds existed all over Europe, especially in the more cut-off mountainous regions. Wild oxen likewise, the ox being much more usual as a beast of burden, especially shackled to a plough, than a horse.

Hyenas are another matter. From their behaviour as scavengers, and perhaps the low-slung carriage of their hind legs, they were universally regarded as untrustworthy and grave-robbers, even to Europeans who had never seen them. Even as recently as the 1950s, the *New Universal Encyclopaedia* refers to them as 'ugly and of repulsive appearance'. It also claims they are 'morose and cowardly', so the Medieval construct took a long time to disappear! Since the species is found in Africa and Asia, this does not help us narrow down the territory of Prester John.

Tigers bring us squarely back to Asia, from the Caucasus to Sakhalin. They were used from time to time to provide entertainment in animal fights in the Roman arena, but more usually in animal versus animal displays rather than tigers versus men (with all due respect to Russell Crowe and an awful lot of CGI in *Gladiator*!). They were very rare in western Europe, which may be one reason why they are virtually non-existent in Medieval heraldry and even as late as the seventeenth century, Edward Topsell in his *History of Four-Footed Beasts* believed all tigers to be female and that they copulated with the wind!

The white and red lions are probably variations of the same species. They were no longer found in Europe by the twelfth century, but were common in both Africa and Asia, so we still cannot narrow down Prester John's frontiers with any degree of certainty. Because of its association with power and strength, the lion in the Middle Ages is the king of the beasts and, appropriately, the most common animal in heraldry.

The white bears referred to by Prester John are intriguing. The bear had once roamed extensively over Europe and in the twelfth century were common in Asia and some parts of North Africa. The Himalayan bear could be found in India, the Malayan in modern Malaysia and the Syrian type in the Middle East. A popular animal in the bestiaries of the twelfth and thirteenth centuries, it was usually portrayed as a mother cleaning her cubs with her tongue. Bear-baiting, duels between chained animals and dogs, was first mentioned in England in the reign of Henry III, but did not become popular until the sixteenth century. It is the colour white that causes confusion in the Prester John letter. All the varieties known in Asia, Africa and Europe were brown or black. The first known reference to a polar bear comes from the court of the Holy Roman Emperor Frederick II in 1245 when he swapped a giraffe for the bear with al-Kamal, the Egyptian sultan. Four years earlier, to show his respect to a fellow king, Hakon IV of Norway sent a 'pale bear' to Henry III of England. It is not clear whether this was actually a polar bear or a light-furred variant (not uncommon) of the European brown bear. There were probably bears still roaming the more inaccessible parts of Britain then, but the sight of this white animal, tethered outside the Tower of London, with a chain long enough for it to catch fish in the Thames, must have been extraordinary.

Then, Prester John's list of animals starts to get silly! In the Medieval bestiary, the griffin was believed to be part lion, part eagle, a combination of the king of the beasts and the king of the birds. The feathers were usually black, white and red and Herodotus wrote that griffins lived in high mountains in India. They dug gold and built their nests with it. The animal's claws changed colour in the presence of poison and they fed on men and horses. The chronicler Huon of Bordeaux described such a beast – 'His beak was marvellously great, his eyes as great as a basin and more redder than the mouth of a furnace and his talons so great and so long that fearful it was to behold him.' The griffin was common in Medieval heraldry.

Lamias were a curious mixture of women with prominent breasts and four-footed animals with claws to the front feet and cloven hoofs to the back. They hissed like dragons and could change shape. It is just possible that rare sightings of African gorillas gave rise to these creatures, although in central European folklore, they were regarded as female vampires, sucking the blood of children in particular. The name itself comes from Greek mythology – Lamia was one of the many mistresses of Zeus.

The Metacollinarium has no explanation in modern zoology, nor anything in the Medieval bestiary either. The word only occurs in the Prester John letter. Yllerons were large birds the size of eagles, with fire-coloured plumage and razor-sharp feathers. They lived for sixty years, laid two eggs and sat on them for forty days before they hatched. At the end of their lives, they drowned themselves in the sea. The forty days has echoes of Christ's time in the wilderness, according to the New testament, and to the obligatory days service under the feudal system in Medieval western Europe. All in all, they sound suspiciously like the phoenix, an Arabian and Egyptian myth. In fact, the phoenix itself, rising from the ashes of its nest burnt by the sun's rays, is also included in the fauna of Prester John's empire.

Tensevetes and cametennus, like metacollarium, defy explanation, but the white merules may be an albino variant of the blackbird (*turdus merules*) or crow. We then have a list that would have made a kind of sense to the literate recipients of the letter. Wild man is an extremely generic term and could mean anything, but in European mythology, the woodwoses were shaggy-haired creatures who lived in forests. They could not speak, stole women and ate unbaptized babies. They were common in heraldry, especially as supporters of shields, and a disaster occurred in 1392 when Charles IV of France took part in a pageant as a wild man, his suit and those of his courtiers made of flax and pitch. One of these caught fire and four men burned to death. The woodwives were the wildmen's female counterparts, able to transform, like Walt Disney witches, from old hag to nubile nymphet in an instant. Centaurs, fauns and satyrs were all creatures from Greek and Roman mythology, but horned men, one-eyed Cyclopses (again, Greek), 'men with eyes before and behind', pygmies and 'forty-ell' (60 feet) giants took some believing. In case he had missed anything out, Prester John claimed that 'nearly all living animals' roamed his kingdom.

The letter then lists fifteen nations, subject peoples who all owed allegiance to the Prester. They were all cannibalistic and Alexander the Great had met them during his conquest of Persia in the fourth century BC and had imprisoned them behind a mountain range in the north of the empire. They were unleashed against Prester John's enemies rather as Hannibal had unleashed his elephants to terrify the Romans. The crucial difference is that the cannibalistic peoples ate the Prester's enemies before being rounded up and taken back to their mountain cages. There was an element of the end of days, the Apocalypse, in the letter – 'These ... nations will burst forth from the four quarters of the earth at the end of the world in the times of the Antichrist and overrun all the abodes of the saints as well as the great city Rome.' The eternal city would be given to Prester John's son, along with all Italy, Germany, the two Gauls, Britain and Scotland. 'We shall also give him Spain and all of the land as far as the icy sea.'

All this is a quaint mixture of Roman history and perhaps even Viking exploration. The two Gauls were the Cisalpine and Transalpine areas as the Romans divided the territory in Julius Caesar's time. Britain is divorced from Scotland because the Roman province of Britannia only extended to Hadrian's Wall. The concept of 'all Italy' and 'Germany' sounds very modern; Italy would not become a single nation until 1861, Germany, ten years later. The icy sea may refer to the north Atlantic, the frozen islands which the Viking Lief Eriksen had navigated over a century and a half before the Prester John letter was sent. There was no cause for undue alarm, the letter said, because the fifteen nations would be destroyed by fire from heaven, 'according to the words of the prophet'. There is no explanation of this. To Muslims, the prophet was Mohammed; to Christians, any of the dozens who littered the Old Testament.

The letter then describes the natural phenomena of Prester John's empire. As with the Biblical Canaan, the land 'streams with honey and is overflowing with milk'. There were no scorpions, snakes, nor frogs with their irritating croaks. The River Indus is the only recognizable geographical feature in the entire letter and gave India its name. It rises in the Tibetan Himalayas and flows south-west to a delta in the Arabian Sea. It is 1,800 miles long and trade caravans to and from Mongolia crossed it. The river was recorded in the context of Alexander the Great's campaign against the Persians, but only Prester John claims that it encircles Paradise, the Garden of Eden. Emeralds sparkled along its banks, as did sapphires, carbuncles, topazes, onyxes, chrisolites, beryls and sardius – all the jewels of the Orient that John Mandeville would catalogue (probably using this letter as his source) nearly 200 years later.

On a practical note, the Prester John missive tells us that all kinds of pepper grow in his lands and that this is traded for corn, bread, leather and cloth. Since *piper nigrum* is native to the East Indies, this had a ring of truth to it, but the Assidos plant went way beyond that. It was worn (probably in an amulet) and warded off evil spirits. This was not unusual; there were several folkloric herbs used in white witchcraft across Europe, but where Assidos was unique was that it forced evil spirits to state their name and business!

Three days journey from the earthly Paradise that John Mandeville would write about, a spring bubbled from the foothills of Mount Olympus. Here, we have a strange mixture of mythology. Several mountain ranges were called Olympus, but most of them were in Greece or Macedonia and one of them was the traditional home of the Greek gods. This had no links, of course, with the Garden of Eden of the Old Testament. The waters of the stream changed flavour every hour and anyone who drank from it three times would never become tired or become any older than thirty. The stones in the stream, Nudiosi, acted as a sight restorative and as a prevention of blindness. Just looking at one of these stones improved vision enormously.

The Prester John Letter is the origin of the waterless sea of John Mandeville, 'consisting of tumbling billows of sand never at rest'. Nobody could cross this sea, which threw up very tasty fish on its beaches. Various travellers, especially the poetic ones, equate endless deserts with oceans; there are no landmarks for miles and the sand is constantly shifting. Not for nothing are camels called the ships of the desert. Just as there was a sea of sand, so there was a river. The stones in it vanished when they reached the sea and it was only possible to cross the river on four days of any given week.

The plain that lay between the sandy sea and the mountains was a place of pilgrimage. Christians and wannabe Christians would find their sins forgiven here, as if they had gone to Rome or Jerusalem. The shrine itself was in the form of a mussel-shell, which may be a garbled version of the symbol of Santiago of Compostella in northern Spain. With the removal of the Muslims of the Ummayid caliphate from the area, the supposed site of St James landing in Spain became free for pilgrims to visit and after Jerusalem and Rome, it became *the* place for pilgrims to find grace. Prester John's shrine was of stone and large enough to hold a man who stood bare-footed in four inches of water until a fountain played over his head in a form of baptism. The sick were cured instantly.

With a nod perhaps to the legendary wealth of King Solomon, there was an underground stream in Prester John's country that contained precious stones. The earth opened for short periods so that the water could be reached and little boys were trained to stay under the surface for three days to collect the gems. This may be linked with various parts of the world where children dive for pearls without any modern breathing apparatus; the earliest known examples of this are in ancient India and the Persian Gulf.

In the high country lived worms called salamanders. These lizards, found frequently in Medieval heraldry 'can only live in fire' and they built cocoons like silk worms. It was this silk that was woven by the ladies of the Prester's court into his regal robes. Aristotle describes these animals and later writers believed they could operate the bellows of blacksmiths' forges. They were generally believed to be poisonous, but since Prester John tells us that there were no poisonous creatures in his domains, this is not mentioned.

The descriptions of the Prester going to war and travelling around his kingdom were to be repeated by Mandeville – crosses led the armies, not banners, and vast numbers of troops defended them. The plain cross of Calvary was carried in everyday movement in peacetime, as well as gold and silver bowls filled with earth, as a reminder of the dust to which we must all return.

The Prester's palace followed the design of Thomas the Apostle (see later) for the Indian king, Gundoformus. The roof and ceiling was made of ebony which cannot burn. Two golden apples shone over the gables and the gates were decorated with huge carved snakes to protect against poison. Portals, floors and furniture were made of ivory, amethyst and crystal. Onyx was used for the area where jousting took place to increase the courage of the combatants. In front of the palace was the most remarkable of all Prester John's belongings, a magic mirror guarded day and night by 3,000 men. By looking into it, the Prester could see what was happening in every region under his rule.

His courtiers were of the highest order, including 62 dukes and 256 counts and marquesses. Twelve archbishops sat on his right at the high table, with twenty bishops on his left. The patriarch of St Thomas, the Sarmatian Protopope and the Archpope of Susi were there too. This reflects the prominence in the east of the Greek Orthodox Church, which, while Christian, differed from the western version and paid no attention to the pope in Rome. This is why Prester John letters were sent to both Alexander III and Manuel Comnenos, representing the different sides of the Christian coin.

Prester John's people, with their abundance of milk and honey, had no poverty, no crime, no adultery, no sin and no envy. All were welcome to his domains and every year, everyone made a pilgrimage to ruined Babylon and to the burial place of Daniel the prophet. In the Old

Testament, Daniel was bracketed with Noah and Job as one of the great figures of Hebrew history. He was believed to have been taken prisoner by Nebuchadnezzar and brought in chains to Babylon, where his visions of the future and interpretation of dreams led to his torture and persecution, both in a furnace and a lions' den. The spurious Book of Daniel, which was accepted as a genuine account in the twelfth century, foretells the collapse of the Persian empire, the rise of Alexander and the coming of Jesus Christ. The problem for Prester John's people was getting to the site. 'Tyri and devilles' guarded the way and since the 'devilles' were serpents, we are once again in the realms of the Old Testament.

There is nothing to suggest that any of the three recipients of the Prester John letter (and there may once have been more) believed all or any of what it said. It was however, an age of miracles. All over Europe, shrines existed to an army of saints whose curative powers were accepted implicitly. The newest of them, which would become the principal English shrine after 1171, was Canterbury, the site of Thomas Becket's murder. And less than fifty years after Alexander III received the letter, between thirty and forty thousand children from France and Germany walked to the Holy Land to win Jerusalem back for Christ. We have no evidence that any of them got there, but they and most of the people who watched them pass, believed that God was with them; he would part the sea and send Jerusalem's walls crashing down. All over Medieval shrines in this period were the crutches of cripples, a symbol that they could now walk thanks to the holy intervention of some saint or another. The whole basis of the Medieval Christian faith, both east and west, was that Christ was the son of God and that he returned from the dead. Seas made of sand and men with eyes in the back of their heads were as nothing compared with that.

It was twelve years before Pope Alexander replied to Prester John's letter. To be fair, he had his hands full with constant threats from Barbarossa and the rival antipopes (by 1172, Callistus III). The plague hit Italy almost as soon as

Barbarossa smashed his way into the Vatican in 1167 and the emperor limped home with his ailing army, taking the pestilence with him. His puppet pope, Paschal, was kicked out by the ever-fickle Romans and Alexander was reinstated.

There was a reconciliation between pope and emperor on 23 July 1177. Barbarossa, never good at grovelling, nevertheless knelt to kiss Alexander's feet, but the pope raised him up with a generous 'Son of the Church, be welcome'. Alexander had been in exile for ten years and for eighteen had put up with a schismatic church. Now it was time for other matters – and one of these was the belated response to Prester John.

Alexander's doctor, Philip, had just returned from a pilgrimage to the Holy Land and while there, he had met a representative of the Prester who told him that the mighty king was a Nestorian Christian. Nestorius was the bishop of Constantinople in 428 and held the view that Jesus Christ was two people and had two natures. He did not take human form and did not suffer on the cross as conventional Christians believed. This was heresy and Nestorius found himself overthrown, excommunicated and exiled to Egypt, where he died in 435. Much like the Bogomils of what is today Romania and the Cathars of the south of France, this heresy had an appeal to philosophers and peasants alike. Nestorianism spread throughout Syria, Persia, India and even China, which would explain its links with Prester John who, it was generally believed, ruled some or all of these countries. By the twelfth century, the heretical aspect seems to have softened and the Nestorians were tolerated by the western Church rather as Greek and Russian Orthodoxy was. This was especially true in that Philip's acquaintance, whoever he was, told him that Prester John wanted to build a church in Rome and an altar at the Church of the Holy Sepulchre in Jerusalem.

This offer of solidarity, rather than the Prester John Letter itself, was seen by Alexander as a chance to increase his prestige as God's lieutenant on earth, which is why, in September 1177, he sent Philip back to the Holy Land, presumably Jerusalem itself, with a letter of friendship for

Prester John. And then, the trail goes cold. There is no more mention of Philip, his second pilgrimage or any contact with the Prester. Bearing in mind the risks involved in such a journey and the elusiveness of Prester John, that is hardly surprising.

The general consensus today is that the Prester John Letter was a forgery. It is explained by some historians as a ruse, perhaps from the Vatican itself, to launch yet another crusade to win back Jerusalem. But there are a number of arguments against that. Of the three known recipients, only one, Frederick Barbarossa, actually went on crusade. He was drowned in June 1190, crossing a river on his way to join Philip of France and Richard the Lionheart in Outremer. With the internal problems that Alexander faced, the launch of another crusade for the Holy Land was probably the last thing on his mind. Ironically, in the case of Manuel Comnenos, his immediate successor, albeit of a different family, found himself the target of the Christian crusaders (essentially his own people) in 1204. Constantinople was looted and sacked, hundreds of sacred relics with their accompanying gold, silver and precious stones finding their way to shrines, cathedrals and palaces all over Europe. Nowhere in the Prester John letter is there the *specific* offer of a military alliance between his eastern Christians and the West; this was largely in the eyes of the beholder, if not, as we have noted above, the eyes of the letters' actual recipients.

The Prester John letter was translated into Hebrew, among many other languages, and modern research into the linguistics of this has suggested that the forgery may have originated among the Jews of northern Italy or Languedoc in the south of France. The problem with this is that the letter was added to as each copying went on, so it is difficult to know what the *original* actually said. It is also difficult to grasp what the motive of a Jewish scholar would be in creating the myth of Prester John; because the myth was there already.

There is an interesting parallel to the Prester John letter in the writings of Eldad ben Mahli ha-Dani, a ninth century merchant who probably came from Arabia. He claimed to be a member of a Jewish state in East Africa, part of the lost ten tribes of Israel. Ha-Dani's tale was one of adventure, capture, travel and cannibalism, ranging over vast areas from Nubia to Persia and perhaps even to China. His lost tribes are warriors who stay in the saddle from one Shabbos to the next and one of them, the Bnei Moshe, the tribe of Levi, lives in a state of harmony very like Prester John's. There are two harvests a year and no child dies in its parents' lifetime. There is no theft or crime. And of course, they speak perfect Hebrew.

It may be that the passing reference to Jewish tribes in the Prester John letter, was deliberately written to refute Ha-Dani's claims, which were believed by a number of Jewish scholars to be true.

But to trace the origins of the story of Prester John, we have to go back to the Bible.

Richard Denham

Prester John

CHAPTER NINE: SON OF

THE MAGI

Everyone in Christendom knew their names. They were Balthasar, Caspar and Melchior and they came out of the East. The nineteenth-century carol extolled the fact – 'We three kings of Orient are'. They were carrying gifts for the newly-born Jesus and they were prepared to travel far, navigating by the stars.

The Gospel of Matthew in the New Testament tells us that wise men – the Latin is magi (masters in the sense of scholars) – first went to Herod, the king of Judea, explaining why they had come; a bright star had led them. Herod, as suspicious of strangers as he was of potential rival kings, sent them on and told him to report back to him where the boy-child was so that he could worship him. In the stable at Bethlehem, they found him and made their offerings of gold, frankincense and myrrh.

Then the dreams started. The Bible, Testaments Old and New, are full of them – visions and portents were the stuff of Hebrew legend as they were of most ancient peoples. The dream told the magi not to return to Herod, so 'they returned into their own country another way'.

There is no mention of the magi, or of Christ's birth,

113

in Mark's Gospel, but the doctor, Luke, describes it, stressing the adulation of the local shepherds rather than foreign kings. The Gospel of John does not cover the birth of Christ at all. So of the four books of the New Testament, only one refers to the magi who have become such an integral part of the 'Christmas story'. The allegorical importance is obvious. Christ was a king for all men, irrespective of wealth, education or social class. So the magi knelt in the stable with the shepherds. They were also not local, but from 'lands afar', attesting to the universal significance of Christ as the Son of God.

Nothing more is known of these three, although we possibly know where they are buried. Helena was the first wife of Constantinus I and the mother of Constantine the Great. Legend has it that she was an innkeeper's daughter but it is a fact that she was abandoned by her husband in 292 and only returned to public life when her son was declared emperor in 306. She was baptized a Christian six years later and it was her influence that persuaded the emperor to adopt Christianity as the faith of the empire, replacing the old pantheon of gods. In 326, she visited Jerusalem and Bethlehem long before such pilgrimages became *de rigeur* for Europeans, rich and poor alike. A keen student of the Bible, Helena claimed to have found innumerable holy sites and founded churches in many of them. Among the relics she uncovered were the cross on which Christ was crucified and the bodies of the magi.

Interestingly, one definition of the word 'magic' which is linked to the magi is 'the practice of attempting or pretending to control events by non-rational processes'. There was, of course, nothing logical or rational about Helena's finds. The true cross, carried later by the crusaders in battle and lost to Salah-ed-Din on the Horns of Hattin in 1187, was nothing of the sort. There are so many claims by shrines, cathedrals and kings to own the cross, that collectively, they would fill a forest. It is no more logical that the three magi should have been buried in the Holy Land, bearing in mind they came from much further east.

Be that as it may, no one questioned such things, either in the fourth century or the twelfth and an entire pilgrimage industry was built around the acquisition of such relics, cathedrals and bishops vying with each other for ownership. Helena, in her day, was the Augusta, the emperor's mother; no one would have challenged her findings. The three bodies ended up in Milan, almost certainly via Constantinople. Constantine's city, where Helena lived in her later years, owned the head of John the Baptist (St Jean d'Angely in France said they had it too!); the lance used to spear Christ on the cross; the body of St Paul and the prophet Samuel and, by the end of the fifth century, had more relics than any other site in Christendom. It may be that the buying, selling and 'swapping' of holy bones explains the three kings' arrival in Milan; one account says that Eustargius, the fourth-century bishop of Milan, acquired them. The present cathedral, magnificent though it is, was not begun until 1386, but it is on the site of an earlier building, originally a Roman basilica which became the coronation site of the kings of Lombardy and the later Roman emperors.

The cathedral's contents, including the lavish tombs of the magi, did not escape the eagle eyes of Frederick Barbarossa. Engaged in a war as he was with Pope Alexander III and various Italian princedoms, he invaded Milan in 1162 on his way to Rome. The magi, gilded tombs and all, were transported to Cologne, where the archbishop gratefully received them; relics of this calibre brought in the pilgrim trade and a great deal of money.

Technically, the removal of holy bones was called translation and it involved a lot of ceremony and protocol. In reality, it was straight theft, although various Byzantine emperors topped up their coffers from time to time by selling off surplus relics to the highest bidder. As late as the fifteenth century, by which time the Portuguese were starting to look for Prester John in Africa, Joos van Ghistele, a seasoned pilgrim, carried with him stones that had been in contact with the magi tombs at Cologne, in the hope that should he discover the Prester or at least his land, he could present them as a goodwill gesture. Since Cologne was one of four major pilgrimage sites in Europe – the others were Canterbury (after 1171), Santiago de Compostella and

Rome – thousands of people prayed at the magi shrine every year.

A new shrine was built for the three in the early thirteenth century. Designed by Nicholas of Verdun, who was probably trained at the abbey of St Denis near Paris, it was presented by the emperor Otto IV, Barbarossa's successor, and the emperor himself is carved in gold on one side of the reliquary, kneeling before the Virgin and Child. There, too, are the magi themselves, with their respective gifts of gold, frankincense and myrrh.

The Gospel of Matthew does not name the magi; nor does it specify their number. We have simply made the assumption based on the three gifts that they brought. The names Melchior, Caspar and Balthazar, with various spellings, occur for the first time in a Greek text written about 500AD. Later writers and, more especially, artists, added their own physical characteristics. So, for example, the monk Bede, from Northumbria, in the ninth century describes Melchior as the eldest of the three 'an old man with white hair and a long beard'.

According to the various traditions that built up, Melchior was a king of Persia and the gold be brought symbolized Christ's role as an even greater king. Nowadays the trend is to see the three as holy men and astrologers rather than kings, but this rather takes away the symbolism; surely, Christ's majesty is enhanced by being knelt to by a king rather than a magician whose dubious star-gazing skills were always equated by some as charlatanism and sleight of hand, as with a modern magician.

If Melchior was the king of Persia, Caspar was accepted as ruler of India. The name perhaps comes from the ancient Greek word for treasurer and Caspar's route to Bethlehem was hinted at by the chronicler John Of Hildersheim in the fourteenth century who claims that he passed through Taxila (now in the Rawalpindi province of the Punjab) on the silk road. Other traditions have him as Gondophares, whose name appears as 'Gondoforus' in the Prester John letter. Gondophares, of Indo-Pathian origin, ruled from 21 to 47AD. His name is an epithet, rather like Genghis Khan and means 'may he find glory'. Some accounts say that Caspar was born in Pirarom in Kerula, India; the town's name means 'birth' and the links with Christ on this score are obvious. In 1448, Andreas Walsperger from Salzburg produced his Mappemunde, map of the world, probably made in Konstanza at the mouth of the Danube. On it, he marked '*hic rex casper habitavit*' (here King Caspar lived) referring to the Golden Chersonese, the Malay peninsula. Caspar was presumed to be the middle magus in terms of age, with an auburn beard.

The youngest was Balthazar, traditionally king of Arabia. Bede describes him as 'of black complexion with a heavy beard' and straightaway we are in the realms of racial confusion. Living all his life as he did in Jarrow and Wearmouth, it is very unlikely that the churchman ever saw anyone with differently coloured skin. So the mid-brown of the Arabs (assuming that Balthazar was Arabian) became the black of Africa and various artists, particularly in the sixteenth century Renaissance, followed the idea. That in turn brought some philosophers back, at the time, to a priest-king somewhere in Africa, beyond the Mountains of the Moon. Balthazar brought myrrh, a highly sought-after and expensive herb associated with death and high-status burials, foretelling Christ's fate on the cross.

The magi met up, say various versions of the vague story, in December 54AD. They all died, at ridiculously advanced ages, the following month. Caspar was 109; Balthazar 112 and Melchior, 116.

Very little about the magi in the Christmas story makes sense. Various Christian and Bible blogs online today contend that it was perfectly credible for eastern scholars ('kings' is now rejected) to look for heavenly portents for the birth of a foreign king, but of course, it was not. Astrology was a vital tool of government for centuries – Elizabeth I of England made few key decisions without consulting her magus, Dr John Dee. But astrologers predicted futures and read auguries for their *own* people, not somebody else's. The supposed date of Christ's birth, 25 December, is highly suspicious. It coincides with the Roman mid-winter solstice of Saturnalia and was already regarded as a holy day throughout the empire. Since the ever-vengeful Herod ordered the slaughter of all innocents under two years old rather than newly-born, it is possible that the magi were ludicrously late anyway and, if they visited at all, found a toddler in his father's carpentry workshop rather than a baby in the manger. There is only one account of the coming of the magi, in the Gospel of Matthew, and since that was probably written soon after 66AD, it may be the incident was motivated by the much-heralded visit of Tiridates, king of Armenia, to the court of the emperor Nero in Rome that year.

But we are not concerned with the factual history of the Bible, which is as notoriously unreliable for the New Testament as it is for the Old. What matters is the myth that grew up about the magi and their links with Prester John. This is why Joos van Ghistele carried the stones that had touched the magis' shrine at Cologne in his search for the Prester, because he was believed to be descended from one of them. All this brings us full circle to the Mongols and the Nestorian Christians of the east.

In 1243, two years before the Franciscan Giovanni de Carpini set out on his missionary trip to the east, the travelling chronicler Sempad the Constable wrote a letter from Samarkand, magical city of carpets, silks and fountains. He was an Armenian nobleman who spent most of his adult life as an ambassador and diplomat. He had been to the Mongol capital of Karakorum, then a brand new city built on the steppe from 1235 and although William of Roubrouck and Carpini were fairly disparaging of the place, it still represented the zenith of the power of the Golden Horde, yet to be reached under Kubilai Khan. What struck Sempad was the Christian church there, as well as the one he had seen in Samarkand.

'Tangut,' he wrote, referring to the area west of the Gobi Desert and north of the Hsi-Hsia empire of the Chinese, 'which is the land from whence came the three kings to Bethlehem to worship the Lord Jesus which was born. And know that the power of Christ has been, and is, so great, that the people of that land are Christians and the whole of [Kara-Kitai] believe these three kings.'

So, rather than the specifics of Persia, India and

Arabia, Sempad puts the origins of the magi further east still, in territory that the Mongols had already overrun by the time he got there and twenty years before the Prester John letter arrived. The theory runs that the Naiman and Keraite tribes in Tangut were descendants of the magi and that the magi, by virtue of the Bethlehem experience, became Christian. To'oril, who took the name Ong Khan or perhaps Genghis Khan himself, were the living descendants of these mystic easterners who had found Christianity and this was the real Prester John.

This in turn linked with the missionary zeal of Thomas the Apostle. 'The *Acts of Thomas*,' writes the American academic Harold W. Attridge, 'is obviously a work of fiction.' This is a pity because it places it in the same context as John Mandeville and the wilder extremes of other writers who probably never left their own firesides. It tells the story of Thomas – often referred to as Didymus (the twin) or Doubting Thomas after his questioning of the reality of the resurrection – who travelled, after the crucifixion, to India. Taken at face value, the disciples were at a loss after Calvary. The reappearance of Christ in the resurrection reaffirmed their faith but in essence, they were members of a quasi-legal sect in an empire run by Romans and among a people (the Jews) who had rejected Christ entirely. They took it upon themselves to spread the Gospel, taking Christ's teaching to the heathen.

The document itself, 171 verses which have been researched diligently by Hebrew scholars and others, probably dates from the fifth or sixth century, building on earlier accounts. There is no disputing the fact that *somehow*, whether via Thomas or not, Christianity *did* reach the East about this time and it became somewhat divorced from mainstream Christianity to become the Nestorian Church. The Jews of Abyssinia had followed a similar path, losing touch with mainstream Jewish theology. This explains the various references to the patriarch of St Thomas and the stage was set for the first known appearance of the legendary king himself, or so it was generally believed, in Rome in 1122.

Twenty-seven years earlier, Pope Urban II had

reached a crusade, a holy war against the Muslims who had taken Jerusalem and the various Christian shrines of Outremer, much to the dismay of pilgrims who were no longer allowed to visit. The Muslims, specifically the Seljuks, were also busy slaughtering merchants whose trade caravans slogged along the spice and silk routes to the east, long before Vasco da Gama and Christopher Columbus tried to find another way. Urban's call to arms seems oddly timed to us today – 1095 was no worse a time for Christian travellers than any other in the previous half-century, but cleric and knight alike were stirred up by the anti-Islamic horror stories of Peter the Hermit, a religious fanatic and eccentric who wandered Europe firing up the great and good. Crusades were potentially good business for anyone intent on carving a reputation or even a mini-kingdom for themselves. The pope himself absolved men in advance; it was not against God's law to kill the infidel, so any amount of slaughter in Outremer was justified. It was three years before a genuine army could be raised, but when it was, led by the Frenchman Godfrey de Bouillon, it was a miraculous success from the crusaders' point of view. With Christ's cross on their surcoats, their banners and their shields, they attacked Jerusalem with shouts of '*Deus Io Vult*' (God wills it) and, according to one eyewitness, waded up to their spurs in blood.

The problem was that the Latin Kingdom of Jerusalem now had to be held together by the Christians, surrounded as Outremer was by a hostile sea of Islam. The bizarre orders of chivalry, the Templars and the Hospitallers, were set up to protect Christians and Jerusalem itself, but it was an uphill struggle and increasingly, the West looked for some sort of salvation from elsewhere. That elsewhere was the East. If only a Christian state, led by a powerful Christian king, could be found, Islam could be destroyed in a deadly pincer movement.

Enter the Patriarch John who visited Rome in 1122. Three years earlier, on 28 June 1119, Roger of Antioch drew up his forces against a much larger Muslim army led by Il-ghazi (the warrior). Ghazi's scouts had told him exactly where Roger was and approximately how many men he had. The crusader was hacked down, a Muslim scimitar slicing through his nose to his brain and the priest beside him, carrying a portion of the True Cross, died too. The Christian accounts swore that God avenged this; the Muslims nearly killed each other scrabbling for the precious stones that the Cross was studded with. The locals, at least those who could read Latin, christened the battleground *ager sanguine*, the field of blood. Other losses followed.

In 1122, the pope was Calixtus II, formerly Archbishop Guido of Vienne, a politician related to French, English and German royal houses. That year, a more important embassy arrived from Henry, the Holy Roman Emperor and this was another crisis point in the long and bitter running feud between pope and emperor that we have met already. Calixtus also had to keep his wits about him in the context of the squabbling Frangipani and Pierleoni families, who, in nascent Mafia-style, were fighting each other for control of Rome. The papacy often got in the way. While Calixtus was negotiating the Concordant of Worms with the emperor (which would, for a while, lead to peace in Europe) Patriarch John of the Indian Church of St Thomas bent his ear on other matters.

John spoke to Calixtus very much along the lines of the description of Prester John's country in the letter of 1167. His capital was Ulna, he said, so huge that it took four days to walk around its walls. The Phison (Ganges) was a vast river that flowed from Paradise and irrigated the whole land. St Thomas's body, in the basilica at Ulna, was of course miraculously preserved and surpassed all the shrines of Rome or indeed anywhere else. The impression was that Patriarch John spoke for the secular area of his kingdom as well as the spiritual. Here was an ally against Islam. Calixtus was as perplexed by Patriarch John's hyperbole as we are today by the claims of the Prester John letter or the account of John Mandeville; except that we have centuries of science and reason on our side and Calixtus did not. He made John swear on holy Gospels in the Vatican that all he said was true, and even then, swore the man to secrecy; no one else was to know of this magical, mystical Christian kingdom in the East.

Probably because of this, there is no mention of Patriarch John's visit in any of the Vatican archives and the reports of it are very much second hand.

In 1145, we have the first written mention of Prester John. Whatever the patriarch said to the pope, whether he himself claimed to be Prester John, or whether he was his archdeacon, there is nothing in writing until that date. Before Salah-ed-Din came to personify the powerful ruling elite of Islam, the warlord who caused most terror was Imad el-Din Zangi, the Turkish atabeg (ruler) of Mosul. He was handsome and brown-skinned with 'beautiful eyes' according to one chronicler. He was also ambitious and quite probably a psychopath – 'like a leopard in character, like a lion in fury ... not knowing any kindness, he was feared for his sudden attacks ... aggressive, insolent, death to his enemies and citizens' – and this was a Muslim account! Like Genghis Khan, he had been brought up amid treachery and betrayal and it left its mark.

It was only because of the size of Zangi's domain – Mesopotamia and Syria – that he made less impact on the crusades than he might have. It was Mosul that was essential to him – the fight against Western Christians was further west and of little interest to him. He broke his word, turned on former allies and did his best to destroy the hegemony of Damascus. While the authorities in that city made an unholy alliance with the crusaders from Edessa (now Urfa in Turkey), the army of Edessa's ruler Joscelin III left their city to come to Damascus's defence. Zangi outmanoeuvred the crusaders and attacked Edessa, hammering it with his siege engines until it fell after four weeks. Hundreds were crushed to death as they crowded for the supposed safety of the citadel on Christmas Eve 1144.

This was a disaster for the crusaders and some historians today see it as *the* turning point in the crusades; never again would the Christian Kingdom of Jerusalem be safe and all it could do was to shrink, the Templars and Hospitallers fighting a rearguard action until 1291 when it fell altogether. In France, the famous and powerful churchman Bernard of Clairvaux wrote, 'The enemy of the Cross has begun to lift his sacrilegious head ... and to devastate with the sword that blessed land, that land of promise'.

News of this disaster was brought to Pope Eugenius III by Hugh, Bishop of Jabula in Syria, who met the pontiff at Viterbo in the autumn of 1145. Eugenius was an odd choice for pope. He had a reputation of being simple, something of a peasant. Even Bernard of Clairvaux did not like him, equating him with 'the poor from the dust' and 'the beggar from the dunghill'. And he should know, because he had taught him! But the pressure was on this simple man to launch the second crusade to win Edessa back.

Writing down everything that was said at Viterbo was the German chronicler Otto von Freisingen who reported that Bishop Hugh had heard of 'one John, king and priest, who dwells in the extreme Orient beyond Persia and Armenia and is, with his people, a Christian, but a Nestorian!' The story was that Prester John had already defeated the Muslim Persians and was due, as per the vague promise of alliance perhaps made by Patriarch John, to come to the aid of the crusaders in Outremer. What had stopped him was the river Tigris because the Prester could not find a suitable crossing place for his troops. He had been hoping for a cold spell, which would freeze the river for long enough to make the crossing; it never happened and he had returned home.

Bishop Hugh went on that this Prester John 'was said to be of the ancient race of those Magi who were mentioned in the Gospel, and to rule the same nations as they did, and to have such glory and wealth that he used only an emerald sceptre. It was from his being fired by the example of his fathers, who came to adore Christ in his cradle, that he was proposing to go to Jerusalem when he was prevented by the cause already alleged.'

This story, improbable as it sounds, was a garbled version of actual events. In 1141, the Seljuk warlord Sinjar was defeated at Katwan near Samarkand by the Kara Kitai, the Mongol people who had ruled north China from 936 to 1122. The Kitai of course gave their name to Marco Polo's version of their lands, Cathay. The warlord equated with

Prester John in the 1140s was Yeliu Tashin. The problem was that he was not a Christian, but a Buddhist.

What we have in the 1140s is an enemy of my enemy. The Muslims had been defeated by a power who could only be Christian – Buddhism was virtually an unknown entity in western Europe. So it followed that Prester John was a reality. No one seems to find it strange that such a powerful warrior who ruled vast territories with his sceptre could not cross a river.

It could only be a matter of time before the crusades – and Christianity itself – were saved by Prester John.

CHAPTER TEN: THE KING

WHO NEVER WAS

Alexander, son of Philip of Macedonia, crossed the Dardanelles, then called the Hellespont, in 334BC. The enemy into whose lands his army marched was the 'great king', Darius, and the lands were the Persian empire. Dazzling victories at Grannicus and Issus drove Darius into a headlong retreat and Alexander set out conquering the outlying areas of the great king's empire. Egypt surrendered without a bow being fired and the conqueror set up his new city of Alexandria and claimed spiritual descent from the Egyptian god Amun.

Three years after crossing the Hellespont, he invaded Babylon through the valley of the river Tigris and smashed Darius' opposition at Gaugemala, capturing Susa and Persepolis and with those cities, most of Darius' fabled wealth. The Persian king was butchered by his own men and, at twenty-six, Alexander was master of the world as the Greeks understood it. No one, before or since, has achieved such success at such an early age or in such a short space of time. Not content with that, Alexander pushed ever eastward, building Greek cities in what would become Afghanistan and crossing the Indus into India itself. It was only his sudden death at thirty-two (some said by poisoning) that brought the whole adventure to a grinding halt.

And then, as always, fiction kicked in. The *Romance of Alexander* was a Greek account of the man's life, first written some time before 338AD. That was already six centuries after the real man's death and not only had facts and actual exploits been forgotten, but new ones were added. Worse, at each re-telling and translation of the *Romance*, additional nonsense and hyperbole crept in. Between the fourth and sixth centuries, the work had appeared in Latin, Armenian, Georgian and Syriac. Later, it turned into Old French, Middle English, Scottish and Irish Gaelic, German, Italian, Russian and Hungarian. It spread to the Arab world too, into Persian, Ethiopic, Turkish, Hebrew and of course Arabic itself. In these later versions, all sorts of magic happened as a matter of course. Alexander met Amazons, the terrifying warrior-women of the ancient world (who just *might* be based on a genuine cult) who removed their breasts to make it easier to draw their bows. He battled centaurs, the half man, half horse creatures of Greek myth. He was tempted, as all folkloric Greeks seem to have been, by the sirens, lethal mermaids who lured careless sailors to their deaths. He conquered Africa, Italy and Britain. His father was not Philip of Macedonia, but the wizard Nectanebus. Dragons roared in the skies above him as he rode east, entering China and building a huge wall to imprison the monstrous giants, Gog and Magog.

In the real world, historians and archaeologists over the last hundred years have worked hard to dismantle this mythology and to recreate what Alexander actually *did*. This is remarkable enough in itself; there really was no need to add more. But mankind has always been fascinated by the magic, the supernatural elements of the world. Modern fiction – be it novels, movies or graphic comics – is deliberately designed to enthral and captivate. Ancient fiction has that facet, too, but added to it were whole shiploads of ignorance, particularly about the natural phenomena of the world. Intelligent, rational men might have doubted the hyperbole of the Alexander Romances; most people did not. Men, women and children who could not read (at any time in the past, the majority) had such fiction read to them or retold in ever more garbled form in their castle solars, or mud huts or around their campfires.

And, of course, in the Christian west at least, the entire faith was based on fiction. The Old Testament, far from being a history of the Hebrews, is one long fabrication. Because the miraculous was always at the hands of God, everyone accepted it. Yes, Moses could part the Red Sea; yes, he could hit the evil pharaoh of Egypt (Rameses II) with plagues of increasing destruction; yes, Noah could survive the Flood in his purpose-built Ark, because all this was achieved through God. The New Testament, of course, has even more miracles; Lazarus back from the dead; water into wine; a gigantic feast from a handful of loaves and a few fish. Above all, a carpenter's son who was really the Son of God and who, like Lazarus, returned from the grave.

It is from these feverish, naïve beginnings that Prester John was born. In a way, it was just more of the same, not written as was John Buchan's novel to entertain teenaged boys, but as a description of the real world just over the horizon. In this book, we have begun with John Buchan and worked backwards, peeling away the additional layers of legend and supposition as we went. Now, let us put all of that into context and see what pattern emerges.

The earliest glimmer of Prester John can just be seen in the *Acts of Thomas* in the third century AD. This of course was only the written culmination of rumours that had been circulating since the crucifixion and resurrection of Christ in Christian beliefs. While Thomas the twin was travelling east, there was an even earlier precedent, rather as John the Baptist and innumerable Old Testament prophets foretold the coming of the Messiah. About thirty-five years before Thomas went to India, wise men came from there, and Persia and Arabia, in search of the infant Jesus. We have no way of proving they ever existed; the sheer paucity of information (the Gospel of Matthew) implies that they probably did not. But the arrival of the magi was a sudden spark to illuminate an eastern world about which the west knew nothing. And Thomas had deliberately gone there, to establish a Christian church and to bring God's light to the darkness of the heathens.

'The modern inheritors of ancient Egypt and Mesopotamia,' wrote S. Tammita-Dolgada in 1994, 'have completely lost touch [with their past]. India, however, has preserved its link ... which remains in the ever-present memory.'

The problem was that outsiders knew nothing of the area to which Thomas travelled and where he, or someone like him, almost certainly had set up a Christian commune by the third century. Pliny the Elder, writing his *Natural History* in 77, said of Taprobane (today's Sri Lanka):

> 'No one had a slave; no one slept beyond daybreak or took a siesta; their buildings were of moderate height; the price of corn never increased; there were no law courts or lawsuits; they worshipped Hercules; the king was elected by the people ...'

We cannot know if Pliny, an erudite scholar, believed this hokum, but his readers certainly did. It sounds like a whinge; Tabrobane has everything that Rome does not. Anybody who was anybody owned slaves in the eternal city. Anybody who was anybody took a siesta. The price of corn was always going up and the whole empire was dogged by greedy lawyers who, as today, made their living from the protracted misery of others. As for kingship, the Romans had deliberately overthrown their kings centuries earlier, only to have them replaced by emperors even more powerful, wilful and dangerous.

Indian civilization was far advanced beyond that of the Middle East, where Thomas came from, and even more so than western Europe. Nalanda in Behar had a famous university that taught mathematics, grammar, mechanics, logic and medicine. The diameter of the world had been calculated there. And this was in 650, five centuries before the first university in Europe was set up at Bologna and nearly six before Oxford came into being.

Information coming out of India before and after Thomas's time usually spoke of trade goods, if only because the tangible evidence for these could be seen in the markets of the Middle East. Indians had been spinning cotton and weaving it since two thousand years before Christ. In Bharuch in the north-west, through which Alexander's armies probably marched, the market stalls groaned with onyx, muslins, porcelain, musical instruments, wine, ointments and perfumes, not to mention beautiful slave girls. In Kolki on the south-west coast, children dived into the blue waters of the sea for pearls. Gems and gold came from the foothills of the Himalayas, sandalwood from the western hills. Coral came from the eastern ocean and crops of all kinds from the Ganges, Taprobane and Burma. This is not the ever more lurid ramblings of a John Mandeville; these accounts are from the ledgers of hard-bitten men, like the Polos centuries later, who traded in the Indian markets every year in the first to third centuries AD.

Rumours of the beautiful artefacts of India spread west. Few ordinary people saw them, still less bought them, but vague stories, enhanced in the telling, of pearl-diving children and elephants and tigers, grew with each generation and made takes of a fabulously wealthy king, dripping with jewels, all the more likely. Thomas's Nestorian Christian church in India did not create the legend of Prester John, but the religious aspect made it all the more palatable to the west; Prester John, when Europeans first heard of him, was *one of us*!

There is one tantalising mention of the priest-king before the Middle Ages proper. Perhaps the most important source for the early Christian church was Eusabius, bishop of Caesarea (today's Kaisari in Turkey). He was writing under Constantine, the first Christian emperor of Rome in the 320s and said, 'The holy apostles and disciples of our Saviour were scattered over the whole world. Thomas, tradition tells us, was chosen for Parthia'. This dichotomy does not pose a problem; Eusabius was probably as ignorant of India and lands to its north as anybody else. Today, Parthia is Iran and Iraq. Among his writings, Eusabius refers to John the Presbyter (priest) of Syria, the tutor of the martyred bishop Papias who in turn had taught Eusabius' own teacher. This rather tortuous link brings us to another of the apocryphal texts, like that of St Thomas, the Epistle of John. It may be that the only link is the name, because there is no suggestion that this John was a king or ruler of any kind. Syria, of course, as well as being home to one of the language translations of the Acts of Thomas, was in the heart of Outremer that would come to dominate the crusades.

From the third century to the twelfth, there is little reference to anyone who might have been Prester John and his absence is telling in itself. We have already discussed the *Alexander Romance* and its spinoffs, but another legend which has a vague bearing is the voyages of Sinbad from the *Thousand and One Arabian Nights*. Probably Persian in origin, like the Alexander stories, the *Arabian Nights* has been told and retold so that its origins are lost. The first known written form dates from the tenth century, but it is clearly based on folkloric collections from Persia, Arabia and Egypt. Sinbad tells of seven voyages in the stories, each more remarkable than the last, involving flying horses, spirits called djinn (as in the genie and the magic lamp) and impossible treasures, many of which recur in the legend of Prester John.

We then come to recorded history, which, sadly, is almost as inaccurate as the fables and rumour we have encountered so far in this chapter. Patriarch John of the St Thomas Christians in India appeared in Rome in 1122 and met the pope, Calixtus II. Thirty-three years later, the chronicler Otto of Freising met Hugh, Bishop of Jabula, in Syria, who had been sent to Pope Eugenius III at Viterbo by Raymond of Antioch, the crusader desperately trying to hold the Christian kingdom of Jerusalem together.

This is the real clue to the importance of Prester John. Thomas's church and the Nestorian Christians in the East had given rise to a myth that somewhere beyond the realms of Islam was a powerful Christian empire that would come to the aid of the beleaguered crusaders. 'From the fabled crusader East,' writes historian Gary Dixon in *The Children's Crusade* (2010), 'came mythic polarities – nightmares of drug-induced atrocities with the Old Man of the Mountain [the Assassin cult] and always-raised, always-dashed messianic hopes with Prester John ...'

We should not doubt the terror caused by the rise of Islam, not once, but in recurring centuries. Some of this was racial ignorance on both sides. Al-Mos'udi in *The Book of Information and Overviews* in the early tenth century, before the crusades began, wrote of Western Christians:

> 'The power of the sun is weak among them ... cold and damp prevail in the regions and snow and ice follow one another in endless succession. Their bodies are large, their natures gross, their manners harsh, their understanding dull and their tongues heavy ... Their religious beliefs lack solidarity and this is because of the nature of cold and the lack of warmth.'

Whereas Mohammed and Jesus Christ had similar ascetic experiences and upset the status quo among their own peoples in the name of their respective gods, their successors (the Muslims in the next generation, the Christians later) spread their respective words with fire and sword. Under various tribes, and families, the Muslims moved out from Arabia, spreading west to the Middle East, including the Christian and Jewish Holy City of Jerusalem. They moved along the coast of North Africa, crossing into Christian Spain and northwards over the Pyrenees into France, only to be stopped by Charles Martel (the Hammer) at Poitiers in 732. In the east, they crossed into Anatolia (today's Turkey), the modern states of Iran and Iraq and the old Persian empire. They pushed as far as Transoxania with its capital of Samarkand and south-east to Kashmir and the Punjab. While it is true that the rise of Islam brought culture and civilization to primitive peoples and that within Islam there was much internecine strife, the Christian west was appalled. Christian Byzantium, personified by the city of Constantine, held out against this alien wave and would do so until 1453 when Mehmet II of the Ottoman Turks destroyed Constantinople. The fall of Edessa, however, in 1141, was every bit as desperate a blow for the earlier crusaders.

The Latin kingdom of Jerusalem, hard won in 1099

by Godfrey de Bouillon, was starting to crack. Raymond of
Antioch asked for help. Pope Eusebius landed the second
crusade. There was no Prester John to ride to the rescue.
He had been on his way, the rumours flew. He had
destroyed the Muslim Samiardi in Persia, had won back the
city of Ecbatana and only the swollen Tigris river had
stopped him from unleashing his mighty forces against the
Muslims now in Edessa.

Confusion upon confusion. The recapture of
Ecbatana was probably the battle of Katwan near
Samarkand, in 1141. The Seljuk Turks had indeed been
defeated and they were then the most powerful force in
Islam. But the man who had beaten them was not Prester
John; he was Yelu Dashi, and he was not even a Christian,
but a Buddhist. Some of the Kara Kitai people who rode
with Dashi were Nestorian Christians and it is vaguely
possible that they carried a cross into battle. It is little, half-
remembered details like this that lead to legends like that of
Prester John.

Then came the letter. Whoever forged this, it was an
extraordinary piece of work. Building on the fanciful myths
of the *Alexander Romance* and mentioning St Thomas and his
Indian church, hope was renewed again. We do not know
whether the letter's recipients – Pope Alexander III, the
Holy Roman Emperor Frederick Barbarossa and Manuel
Comnenos of Byzantium believed it, but the fact that it was
still being translated three hundred years after its arrival and
was produced on that miracle of the fifteenth century, the
printing press, proves that a lot of people did. Something
had gone wrong in the 1140s and the Prester had not
galloped to the rescue of Christian civilization. But that was
then. This was 1165 and the flame still burned.

Frederick II, the Holy Roman Emperor, called
himself *Stupor Mundi*, the wonder of the world, not the most
self-effacing of titles. He had to fight to obtain his crown,
but having done so, set out for the Holy Land in 1228.
Jerusalem had fallen back in 1187 and although Richard
the Lionheart had defeated the Seljuk leader Salah-ed-Din
twice in open battle, he could not take the holy city itself. So
the 'kingdom of Heaven' was shrinking by the time the

wonder of the world galloped to its rescue. To be fair to the man, he succeeded where the Lionheart had failed, not by siege engines and sheer guts, but diplomacy and bribery. He had himself crowned King of Jerusalem, adding to his many titles, but did not stay to hold the fragile kingdom together. He went home.

Enter King David of India, or to be more precise, Subedai of the Reindeer People, the able general of the perfect warrior, Genghis Khan. As we have seen, western involvement with the Mongols was very limited in the early thirteenth century. We have a handful of Catholic missionaries attempting to make contact with the Nestorian church and/or find converts for Rome. A glance at a modern map of 1260 shows the Khanates of the Mongols and the Seljuk held Anatolia (Turkey) side by side but of course the Mongols had swept very rapidly from much further east and they were virtually unknown to Europeans. The chronicler Jacques de Vitry, Bishop of Acre, came back from the fifth crusade that had achieved virtually nothing with news that 'King David' was the son or grandson of Prester John. He was riding for Baghdad and fully intended to recover and rebuild Jerusalem in God's name. All this was wishful thinking and it may be that 'David' was the creation of the shrinking crusader kingdom desperate to revive their chances of survival. Of the five crusades up to 1229, only one, the first, had been successful. The fourth was technically a crusader victory, but it was fought against the fellow Christians of Constantinople and merely resulted in weakening Byzantium further and obtaining a vast number of holy relics to be scattered around Europe.

The geography of Prester John had now shifted in a new direction. Most people who had heard of the man probably saw him as they saw God himself, a venerable, white-bearded ruler, sitting on a diamond-encrusted throne and wearing a crown. His skin was probably white, in that the black men that Europeans had heard about, along with the tiny few that some of them may have seen, could not possibly be Christian.

Genghis Khan looked nothing like that. He was a Tengrist, that is, he worshipped the sky god Tengri and his religion was shamanistic, reliant on signs and portents to divine the future. That said, the Mongols, like the later Muslims, were tolerant of other faiths and it is possible that one of the Great Khan's many wives was a Nestorian Christian. It is against this background of tolerance and of the Mongol Golden Horde sweeping ever further west, that men like Giovani de Plano Carpini and Guillaume de Roubrouck were sent by the pope to spread the word of God.

Two chroniclers from this period told it like it was. But 'like it was' did not appeal. Jean de Joinville was a French knight brought up at the highly literate court of the count of Champagne with its tradition of the balladeers called troubadours and of Arthurian romances. He accompanied Louis IX of France on the seventh crusade in 1241 and became a close adviser to the king. He was commissioned to write a biography of his lord and this became *La Vie de Saint Louis* dedicated to Louis X. It is a highly readable account of the crusades, filled with anecdotes and even humour. The only reference to Prester John is a brief and disparaging one, referring to the king's defeat by Chingiz (Genghis) Khan and probably relates to Ong Khan, who we know became one of Genghis' bitter enemies. There is nothing of the hugely popular ruler of magical lands here, but then, there is no evidence that Joinville ever travelled further east than the Holy Land.

Odoric of Pardenone is different. An Italian Franciscan friar and missionary, he followed in the footsteps of Carpini and Polo, visiting the Balkans and, by 1318, Mongolia. As his party passed through Armenia and Persia, he collected the bones of earlier Christians who had been executed by the Muslims and had them reburied with suitable veneration. He spent over a year in Khanbelik (today's Beijng) at the court of the Great Khan, Yesun Temur, the grandson of Kubilai and great-grandson of Genghis. In his writings, probably intended as a report for the pope, he mentions the Chinese habit of compressing women's feet and the Mandarin fashion for long fingernails. He also saw fishermen using cormorants to catch fish. On his return journey, around 1328, he passed through the lands of Prester John, which may have been Mongolia and all he saw was endless Steppelands; again, no sign of the wonders of the fabled king. He refers specifically to Casan, which, if it was Kazan, was a Tartar stronghold much further west, not far from Moscow.

Marco Polo's version refers to the rift between Prester John and Genghis Khan over the proposed marriage of their children. Affronted even by the suggestion of marriage, Prester John declared war and was ultimately defeated. The historical figure at the centre of all this was the Nestorian Christian leader To'oril. Joinville, Odoric and Polo all follow the same line, as in their way do Carpini and Roubrouck. They use Prester John's name for somebody else, be it Ong Khan, To'oril or Genghis Khan himself, but essentially he is simply a local warlord. If he was not Genghis Khan, then he was a Nestorian Christian defeated by the perfect warrior as he unified the Mongol and Tartar tribes before taking on China.

Had matters ended there, it is likely that the name of Prester John would have been forgotten, but the collapse of the vast Mongol empire changed all that. The Mongols, poised at the gateway to Europe under Genghis Khan, pulled back from further western conquests and by 1313, many of the steppe peoples had become Muslim. It is difficult to comprehend the blow that this caused to the west. To those who believed that the Mongols were actually Christians led by their magical saviour king, at a stroke, that idea was snuffed out. On the other hand, the collapse of Christian Outremer in 1291 meant that there was no *cause celebre* left for Prester John to save. Real or not, the west no longer had need of him in quite the same way. And because of the Muslim conversion of the Mongols, travel eastward was more difficult and dangerous than ever for the west, and the rumours and the fiction could increase.

Enter John Mandeville. Whoever its author was, *The Travels* with their preposterous descriptions of seas of sand, dog-headed people and the precious stones of Paradise, rekindled the legend of fabulous wealth and dazzlingly odd places far away. 'Mandeville' seems to have stolen the accounts of Polo, Carpini and Roubrouck and embellished them with nonsense of his own. The difference is that Genghis Khan and the Mongols now dropped out of the picture. The focus became the three Indias, which included the southern fringe of the Mongol empire as well as the hotter zones that take us into Sri Lanka and the Indian Ocean.

Mandeville's contemporary was John of Hildesheim, a Carmelite Friar who wrote *Historia Trium Regum*, a History of the Three Kings, probably in the 1350s. Hildesheim invented back stories for Melchior, Caspar and Balthazar and took the tale up to the appearance of their shrine at Cologne cathedral. He also covered the most famous descendant of the kings, Prester John, endowing him with an equally fictitious narrative. It did not help the seekers of truth and reality that Wolfram von Escenbach muddied the waters still further with his poem *Parzival*. Von Escenbach, a partially-illiterate knight, possibly from Bavaria, dictated his *Parzival* some time after 1217, so he predated Mandeville by over a century and even Polo and Carpini. Making up elements of the universally popular stories of King Arthur as he went, Essenbach has Prester John as the son of the Grail maiden and a Saracen (Muslim) knight called Feirefiz. Interestingly, bearing in mind the fabulous gemstones associated with the Prester, the Grail is not the cup of Christ's last supper in Escenbach's account but a jewel.

It is difficult to know when exactly the location of Prester John's empire switched to Africa. Perhaps with the inability of missionary priests from the west to find such a fabulous king in Asia (despite the possibilities outlined above) scholars reasoned that 'India', that vague term that was applied all over the place, might include the Horn of Africa, which they called Ethiopia. Joe Thornton in *A Cultural History of the Atlantic World* (2012) suggests that this shift may have happened as early as 1250, but that seems unlikely. Not only were the crusades still in full swing by then, but the Mongols were still on the warpath and William of Roubrouck, for instance, had not yet set out on his mission to the East.

Marco Polo described Ethiopia (as Abyssinia was generally known) as a 'magnificent Christian land' (although he had never been there) and many in the west believed that the Ethiopians would one day invade Arabia across the Straits of Hormuz and bring down Islam in its heartlands. From the first to the sixth centuries, Ethiopia had a large Christian community focussed on its capital, Axum. There were churches here and a tradition of pilgrimage developing at the same time as that to Rome and the Holy Land. At Axum, the tablets of the law, as given to Moses, were believed to have been taken out of Jerusalem and brought south by Menelic, the son of Solomon and the queen of Sheba (Saba in Abyssinia). No one queried this story, any more than they did any other aspect of the Bible and both Solomon and Sheba (who were never the lovers depicted by Hollywood!) were equated with fabulous wealth. Skirting the complicated issue of individuals, however, there is no doubt that Coptic Christians, kicked out of Egypt, did follow the Nile's right bank and settle to the south. In 525AD, the Ethiopian king Kaleb invaded Yemen across the Straits and destroyed a Jewish community at Hemyar.

By the seventh century, the fortunes of Ethiopia had been reversed. An attempt to attack Mecca, the cultural and spiritual heart of Islam, failed in 570. As the Muslim faith grew, Eritrea, to Ethiopia's north, was overrun and Axum as a political entity collapsed. There was anarchy for nearly two centuries until the Zagwe dynasty established law and order and made the Christian faith official. Ironically, it was religion that destroyed the new settlement, because the church authorities said that only a descendant of Menelic could govern and to carry the title of *negus* (ruler). The leader of this revolt was Yerkuno Anlak who claimed descent from Menelic. His descendants, backed by the local variant of the church and the wealth of monasteries, remained rulers until 1855.

The protocol of government was set down in the fourteenth century as the *Kebara Nagast* (the Splendour of Kingship). Successive kings took Biblical names and made it their business to stop any encroachment from Islam. Small wonder that there were those in the west who saw Ethiopia as the kingdom of Prester John and this was reinforced in 1306 when thirty ambassadors sent by the emperor Wedem

Arad visited Pope Clement V. They told him that the patriarch of their church was Prester John. Here, we have the interesting concept of separating church and state. Generally, the legendary king was a priest too (the clue is in the name) yet here, we have an emperor and a senior priest who are clearly two different people.

In the decade that 'John Mandeville' was born, another writer came out with a description of the Prester's kingdom. The work was called *Mirabilis Descripta* and the author was Jordanus, a Dominican missionary from the Catalan region of Spain and he was sent by Pope John XXII to be the first Christian bishop of Quilon (today's Kollan) in India. What Jordanus was doing was revising the church of St Thomas from thirteen centuries earlier and the account he left of Indian customs and rituals was the first to reach the west in such detail. He describes Parsee services, the worship of oxen and the horrendous Hindu practice of *suti*, wives committing suicide on the funeral pyres of their husbands, later outlawed by the British.

Jordanus was the first to define the three Indias, although few people paid much attention. India major ran from Malabar to Cocin; India minor from Sind to Malabar; and India tertia included east Africa. It is in this region that the bishop placed the kingdom of Prester John.

By the fourteenth century, when 'John Mandeville' was writing and by the fifteenth, when Portuguese exploration began, Ethiopia was a successful Christian state on the edge of Islam, still nominally a magic and distant land, now in a continent not fully explored or mapped and where few white men had been. The geography may have shifted, but the legendary existence was largely the same. And the fifteenth century of course saw the westward conquests of the Ottoman Turks and the destruction of Constantinople. It was the old enemy in a slightly different guise and the notion of crusade and Holy War was not yet entirely dead.

The Ethiopian culture was unique. With its own monophysitic brand of Christianity (denying Christ's human existence) and physically cut off by the Red Sea and the Sahara Desert, Ethiopians had developed their own alphabet by the fifth century. It had twenty-six letters and was used largely for liturgical purposes, which explains why, by the eighteenth century, various explorers spoke of an illiterate people governed by a literate church. The culture also produced extraordinary works of art, miniature paintings, book illumination and frescoes, using paint made from vegetable oils sprinkled with gold dust. With the exception of the courts of rulers like Lemba Dengel and Tewodros II, even this had gone by the nineteenth century.

By the 1420s, faced once again with the Muslim threat, various European rulers looked for new ways to reach the East. Henry the Navigator, king of Portugal, took an early lead here, with Vasco da Gama rounding the Cape of Good Hope into the Indian Ocean. In 1487, Piero da Corvilha and Afonso de Pavia were sent by King Manuel on the overland route, travelling up the Nile, to reach the land now equated with that of Prester John. Corvilha got there, but was not allowed to leave. There may have been emotional or practical reasons for this, but it merely enhanced the mystery of the legendary king. He may once have been equated with the hard-riding Golden Horde of the Mongolian steppes; now he sat on his throne (the maps of the time confidently showed) behind the Mountains of the Moon. In 1520, as a result of another trade/alliance initiative, Francisco Alvares arrived in Ethiopia, noted what he saw and wrote *Verdadeira Infomação das Terras do Preste João das Indias* (a True Relation of the Lands of Prester John of the Indies). From that time onwards, as the links between western Europe and Ethiopia strengthened and visits became more commonplace, various Europeans asked their Ethiopian contacts about their mysterious ruler, Prester John. They were met with blank or puzzled looks; no ruler of Ethiopia had ever been called that.

Prester John was kept alive in fictional references for years, but his image was fading. In Shakespeare's *Much Ado About Nothing*, probably written in 1599, Benedick, Lord of Padua, offers to do any service for Don Pedro, Prince of Aragon – 'I will fetch you a tooth-picker now from the furthest inch of Asia, bring you the length of Prester John's foot, fetch you a hair off the great Cham's beard, do you any embassage to the Pigmies.'

The glover's son from Stratford (or whoever wrote Shakespeare!) had definitely read his 'Mandeville'. Prester John's foot reminds us of the people with one large foot which they could use as a sunshade, while in the next sentence, the great Cham is the Great Khan of the Mongols and China. There is no mention here of Ethiopia – Prester John belongs squarely to Asia.

By the late seventeenth century, we can glimpse the beginnings of antiquarian research. The antiquarians were not at all selective, grabbing everything they could about historical topics and writing it all down. It is the collection of data that is important, not the interpretation of it but by 1681, a German orientalist, Hiob Ludolf, in his *Historia Aethiopica* reached the conclusion that there was not, nor had there ever been, any king called Prester John in Ethiopia.

Ethiopia became Abyssinia and the succession of missionaries, diplomats and explorers whom we met in Chapter 3 travelled the land, equally fascinated and appalled by live cattle eating and casual sex. Not one of them found anyone called Prester John; neither was he referred to as a figure from history. The myth of Prester John was not African. It was not even Asian. It grew in the minds of Europeans.

And almost as soon as the Prester had all but disappeared, along with Arthur and Robin Hood and the Old Man of the Mountain, he came back again, phoenix-like, in John Buchan's novel of 1910. Even then, Buchan skirted the issue. The book is not about the priest-king himself, but tangential to him via an object said to belong to him. Other fiction has followed. In 1930, the year in which Ras Tafari was crowned Haile Selassie, *negus* of Abyssinia, Charles Williams wrote *War in Heaven*, a novel which linked von Escenbach's holy grail with Prester John once again. In 1993 historian and crime writer M.J. Trow included the ghost of the legendary king in one of his Inspector Lestrade series, *Lestrade and the Mirror of Murder.* And in 2000, Umberto Eco wrote *Baudolino*, involving the 1165 Prester John letter and the emperor Frederick Barbarossa. Whackier still, the Prester appears in a variety of Marvel comics where his legendary powers fit right in!

A little after 9.30 on the morning of Friday, 30 April 1943, a local fisherman was checking his nets along the beach at Huelva in Southern Spain. He noticed something larger than fish, rolling in with the tide. It was the body of a man. The fisherman reported the grisly find to the police who called in the militia. They transported the corpse to the town and informed the local naval judge.

Spain was a neutral country in the 1940s but most of the rest of Europe was convulsed by the Second World War. Spain's neutrality was paper thin; the country had just come through a bloody and bitter civil war, Fascism against Communism, and General Francisco Franco's side had won. Officially, exhausted and bankrupt Spain kept out of the war, but the new Fascist government was perfectly willing to help the Abwehr, the German Intelligence unit, and the whole country was crawling with spies.

Documents found in a briefcase chained to the body proved that he was a British officer, Captain (acting Major) William Martin of the Royal Marines. In his wallet, he carried a photograph of his girlfriend Pam and two love letters from her. There was also a receipt for an engagement ring that had cost Captain Martin £53 10s 6d (today, in the region of £2,650) from a Bond Street jeweller. Lloyds Bank had been in touch too; Martin had an overdraft of £79 19s 6d (£12,580). More importantly, he carried various letters to key members of both British and American staffs, making it clear through coded messages that the next Allied offensive would be an invasion of Greece and the Balkans, using Sicily as a feint.

Because the body was British, the local vice-consul, Francis Haselden, was informed and he attended the post-mortem held in Huelva on 1 May. It was a hot day and the corpse, having been in the sea for a certain length of time, was smelling to high heaven. Haselden suggested that the two doctors handling the body should call it a day and have lunch. They agreed and gave as the official cause of death 'asphyxiation through immersion in the sea'. Martin was buried with full military honours the next day.

Except that he should not have been. Because he was not and never had been in the military. Neither had he ever been immersed in the sea, except for perhaps half an hour as he was floated off the British submarine HMS *Seraph* on 29 April. He was not a Marine and his name was not Martin. There was no 'Pam' and the engagement ring and debts were phoney.

More importantly, the suggested Allied target of the Balkans rather than Sicily was phoney too. That had been the whole point of the exercise. It was a 'sting' by Royal Naval Intelligence to dupe the Germans into deploying front-line troops in the wrong place. And it worked like a dream. As for William Martin RM, he was actually Glyndwyr Michael, a native of Aberbargoed in Wales who lived as a tramp in north London. He had died by eating rat poison, though whether this was accident or suicide remains unknown.

The macabre tale of Acting Major Martin was written up in a best-selling book by the man who made the whole Operation Mincemeat work, Ewan Montague and was made into a highly successful film eleven years after the war ended. It was called *The Man Who Never Was.*

Which brings us back to Prester John. Throughout this book we have met him – or nearly met him – by any number of phoney names. He was the Patriarch John. He was Ong Khan. He was Genghis Khan. He was Lemba Dengel. And actually, he was none of these. He was Mr Nobody – the King Who Never Was. But just like Glyndwyr Michael, who achieved sadly little during his life and did nothing for the war effort, he did a great deal after his death simply by not being alive at all. He gave countless generations hope. At times during the crusades when the Islamic wave seemed too great to stop, he was there, always distant, always poised, always on his way and never *quite* arriving. But he *was* there. And later, when men looked outward from the narrow, insular world of Medieval Europe, the search for Prester John led them to lands they had not dreamt of, to civilizations they did not know existed. Prester John made them believe that magic was possible, not just the eager schoolchildren who read John

Buchan's gripping novel, but countless adults who wondered whether it was just possible that in the Prester's lands, there really were men with faces in their chests; whether there were people who lived near Paradise and fished in rivers made of sand; whether there could actually be such a place where there was no crime and no poverty, no greed and no envy, all of it presided over by a magical and Christian king with powers unheard of in the world they knew.

This is the legacy and this is the importance of Prester John. He makes us believe, as John Buchan once wrote, that in all of us, no matter how humble, there is something of a king.

Richard Denham

BIBLIOGRAPHY

ASBRIDGE, Thomas, *The Crusades,* Simon and Schuster, 2012

ATTRIDGE, Harold W., *The Acts of Thomas,* Polebridge Press 2010

BARBER, Richard and RICHES, Anne, *A Dictionary of Fabulous Beasts,* Boydell Press 1975

BUCHAN, John, *Prester John,* 1910

DUFFY, Eamon, *Saints and Sinners,* YUP 1997

HAHN, David, *The Tower Menagerie,* Simon and Schuster, 2003

HOTTEN, John Camden, ed., *Abyssinia and its People,* Elibron Classics 2010

KNIGHT, Ian, '*Go To Your God Like a Soldier*', Greenhill Books 1996

MANDEVILLE, John, tr Anthony Bale, *The Book of Marvels and Travels,* OUP 2012

MARSHALL, Robert, *Storm From the East* BCA 1993

MORTIMER, Ian, *The Time Traveller's Guide to Medieval England,* Vintage 2009

NORWICH, John Julius, *The Popes,* Vintage 2012

POLO, Marco, *The Travels,* Penguin Books, 1958

SUMPTION, Jonathan, *Pilgrimage,* Faber and Faber 1975

Times Atlas of World History, Harper Collins 1993

TROW, M.J., *The Adventures of Sir Samuel White Baker,* Pen and Sword 2010

Other titles by BLKDOG Publishing that you may enjoy:

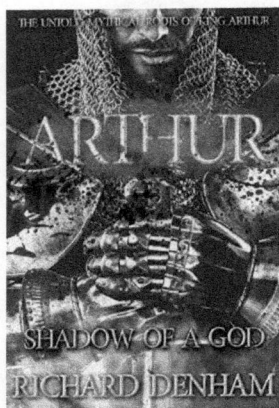

Arthur: Shadow of a God
By Richard Denham

King Arthur has fascinated the Western world for over a thousand years and yet we still know nothing more about him now than we did then. Layer upon layer of heroics and exploits has been piled upon him to the point where history, legend and myth have become hopelessly entangled.

In recent years, there has been a sort of scholarly consensus that 'the once and future king' was clearly some sort of Romano-British warlord, heroically stemming the tide of wave after wave of Saxon invaders after the end of Roman rule. But surprisingly, and no matter how much we enjoy this narrative, there is actually next-to-nothing solid to support this theory except the wishful thinking of understandably bitter contemporaries. The sources and scholarship used to support the 'real Arthur' are as much tentative guesswork and pushing 'evidence' to the extreme to fit in with this version as anything involving magic swords, wizards and dragons. Even Archaeology remains silent. Arthur is, and always has been, the square peg that refuses to fit neatly into the historians round hole.

Arthur: Shadow of a God gives a fascinating overview of Britain's lost hero and casts a light over an often-overlooked and somewhat inconvenient truth; Arthur was almost certainly not a man at all, but a god. He is linked inextricably to the world of Celtic folklore and Druidic traditions. Whereas tyrants like Nero and Caligula were men who fancied themselves gods; is it not possible that Arthur was a god we have turned into a man? Perhaps then there is a truth here. Arthur, 'The King under the Mountain'; sleeping until his return will never return, after all, because he doesn't need to. Arthur the god never left in the first place and remains as popular today as he ever was. His legend echoes in stories, films and games that are every bit as imaginative and fanciful as that which the minds of talented bards such as Taliesin and Aneirin came up with when the mists of the 'dark ages' still swirled over Britain – and perhaps that is a good thing after all, most at home in the imaginations of children and adults alike – being the Arthur his believers want him to be.

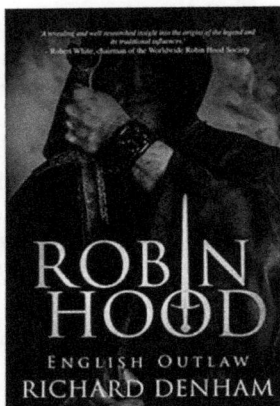

Robin Hood: English Outlaw
By Richard Denham

'A revealing and well-researched insight into the origins of the legend and its traditional influences.' – **Robert White, chairman of the Worldwide Robin Hood Society**

We all have an idea of Robin Hood, England's most famous outlaw: a handsome and hooded woodsman in Lincoln green emerges from the crowd, effortlessly looses his bow at his target and splits another arrow in two to the astonishment of the spectators. We can imagine Robin Hood, but why, and where have our ideas of the man actually come from?

What is most surprising about the legend of Robin Hood and his Merry Men is how much his tales have deviated since they were first conceived. We start almost a thousand years ago with a group of bandits, comical and criminal in equal measure, who despised the Church, kidnapped strangers and waged war on lords and landowners, but astonishingly, and perhaps inexplicably, Robin was destined for greater things. Robin, like his readership, adapted, evolved and changed with the long centuries. We see him turn into a righteous partisan, stealing from the rich and giving to the poor and heroically defending the people from the tyranny of King John until the return of Richard the

Lionheart. Stories that we think are ancient are often less than a century old, politically correct additions from the nascent age of cinema. We find him now a Hollywood heart-throb, with perfect teeth, designer stubble and an almost supernatural skill in combat and romance as he conquers enemies and lovers alike. And, as history always reminds us, the stories we know are rarely the stories that are true.

Robin Hood: English Outlaw gives a fascinating account of the famed rogue, unraveling the layers of legend and myth in search of the man who has always been an enigma. The story of Robin is inextricably linked with the story of England; he shares our greatest achievements, our proudest moments and our darkest chapters.

And this is the enduring legacy of Robin Hood, whether man or myth, whether hero or villain, he *is* part of England's story. We know Robin, the Merry Men and Sherwood Forest; we just don't remember why.

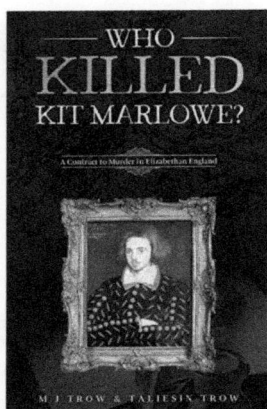

Who Killed Kit Marlowe?: A Contract to Murder in Elizabethan England
By M. J. Trow & Taliesin Trow

Kit Marlowe was the bad boy of Elizabethan drama. His 'mighty line' of iambic pentameter transformed the miracle plays of the Middle Ages into modern drama and he paved the way for Shakespeare and a dozen other greats who stole his metre and his ideas. When he died, stabbed through the eye in what appeared to be a tavern brawl in Deptford in May 1593, he was only 29 and many people believed that he had met his just deserts.

But Marlowe's death was not the result of a brawl. And it did not take place in a tavern. The facts tell a different story, one involving intrigue, espionage, alchemy and the highest in the land.

Born the son of a shoemaker in Canterbury, Marlowe read Theology at Corpus Christi College, Cambridge and was destined for a career in Elizabeth I's new Church of England. But in 1583, he moved to London and wrote dazzling new plays like *Dido, Queen of Carthage, Tamburlaine, the Jew of Malta* and *Doctor Faustus*. He was the 'Muse's darling', 'all fire and air' and the crowds flocked to his dramas at the Curtain, the Theatre and the Rose.

But even before he left Cambridge, Kit Marlowe was recruited into the dangerous and murky world of espionage, perhaps by Nicholas Faunt, secretary to the queen's spymaster, Francis Walsingham. The religious world was split between Catholic and Protestant and there was a price on the queen's head - the pope himself had ordered the assassination of the English whore, the Jezebel, who had betrayed Catholicism. Walsingham's efforts and those of 'intelligencers' like Marlowe, were all designed to keep the queen and her country safe.

Marlowe was a maverick, a whistle-blower, with outspoken views on religion, the government for which he worked and he was critical of the norms of behaviour. Almost certainly homosexual, at a time when that meant execution, he claimed that Christ had a homosexual relationship with John the Baptist. Or did he? Was all that merely propaganda, invented by the ever-growing list of enemies building up by 1593?

This book offers a different interpretation to the death in Deptford. Marlowe knew too much about the Privy Council, the gang of four who effectively ran England under the queen. He openly defied them in his last plays – *the Massacre at Paris* and *Edward II*. And they, in turn, were keen to destroy him – 'His mouth must be stopped' – and stopped it was by a trio of agents operating at the highest level.

The brutal murder of a young playwright at the peak of his powers has intrigued and captivated for over 400 years. This compelling journey through the evidence allows us to know, for the first time, who killed him.

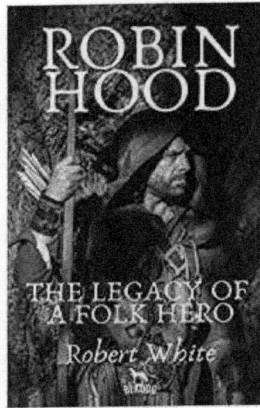

Robin Hood: The Legacy of a Folk Hero
By Robert White

If you thought you knew about Robin Hood... then think again!

Written by Robert White, chairman of the World Wide Robin Hood Society.

Many tales have been told about Robin Hood. The traditional stories of good versus evil and his quest to regain his rightful inheritance are universally appealing. The legend has intrigued generation after generation and everyone has their own personal vision of Robin Hood - a swashbuckling hero; a romantic outlaw; a bandit thief; a fighter of injustice or a benevolent champion of the people. Numerous books have been written by historians trying to untangle the myth, establish his actual existence and speculate on just who he might have actually been. Consequently, the subject of the globally renowned hero of English folklore has become extensively complex but the observations included in this publication should provide a brief overview of some of the key facts, issues and perceptions surrounding Robin Hood.

Robin Hood: The Legacy of a Folk Hero gives a fascinating insight into the numerous aspects of one of the world's most enduring and iconic legends. Robert White discusses interesting facts and titbits surrounding the outlaw, and then reflects on how the Sherwood Forest hero has become a global phenomenon who, over 800 years, evolved into 'the people's champion'. Embark on an journey from the legend's mythical roots to how, across the ages, the tales of Robin and his merry men has developed in many diverse ways that still impact us to this day.

Whatever your opinions and beliefs, this title will reveal just why Robin Hood has become so much more than simply a mythical outlaw of English folklore.

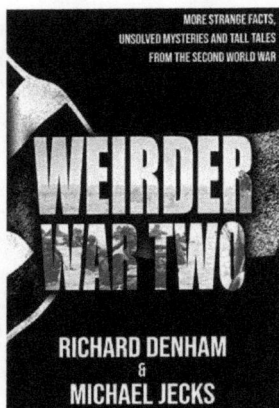

MORE STRANGE FACTS,
UNSOLVED MYSTERIES AND TALL TALES
FROM THE SECOND WORLD WAR

WEIRDER
WAR TWO

RICHARD DENHAM
&
MICHAEL JECKS

Weirder War Two
By Richard Denham & Michael Jecks

*Did a Warner Bros. cartoon prophesize the use of the atom bomb? Did
the Allies really plan to use stink bombs on the enemy? Why did the
Nazis make their own version of Titanic and why were polar bear
photographs appearing throughout Europe?*

The Second World War was the bloodiest of all wars. Mass
armies of men trudged, flew or rode from battlefields as far
away as North Africa to central Europe, from India to
Burma, from the Philippines to the borders of Japan. It saw
the first aircraft carrier sea battle, and the indiscriminate use
of terror against civilian populations in ways not seen since
the Thirty Years War. Nuclear and incendiary bombs
erased entire cities. V weapons brought new horror from
the skies: the V1 with their hideous grumbling engines, the
V2 with sudden, unexpected death. People were
systematically starved: in Britain food had to be rationed
because of the stranglehold of U-Boats, while in Holland the
German blockage of food and fuel saw 30,000 die of
starvation in the winter of 1944/5. It was a catastrophe for
millions.

At a time of such enormous crisis, scientists sought ever
more inventive weapons, or devices to help halt the war.
Civilians were involved as never before, with women taking

up new trades, proving themselves as capable as their male predecessors whether in the factories or the fields.

The stories in this book are of courage, of ingenuity, of hilarity in some cases, or of great sadness, but they are all thought-provoking - and rather weird. So whether you are interested in the last Polish cavalry charge, the Blackout Ripper, Dada, or Ghandi's attempt to stop the bloodshed, welcome to the Weirder War Two!

Click Bait
By Gillian Philip

A funny joke's a funny joke. Eddie Doolan doesn't think twice about adapting it to fit a tragic local news story and posting it on social media.

It's less of a joke when his drunken post goes viral. It stops being funny altogether when Eddie ends up jobless, friendless and ostracised by the whole town of Langburn. This isn't how he wanted to achieve fame.

Under siege from the press, and facing charges not just for the joke but for a history of abusive behaviour on the internet, Eddie grows increasingly paranoid and desperate. The only people still speaking to him are Crow, a neglected kid who relies on Eddie for food and company, and Sid, the local gamekeeper's granddaughter. It's Sid who offers Eddie a refuge and an understanding ear.

But she also offers him an illegal shotgun - and as Eddie's life spirals downwards, and his efforts at redemption are thwarted at every turn, the gun starts to look like the answer to all his problems.

BLKDOG

www.blkdogpublishing.com

www.ingramcontent.com/pod-product-compliance
Lightning Source LLC
Chambersburg PA
CBHW030015290326
41934CB00005B/344